H

ARMAGH GAOL 1971–1986

Hard Time
Armagh Gaol 1971–1986

Raymond Murray

Mercier Press

MERCIER PRESS
PO Box 5, 5 French Church Street, Cork
16 Hume Street, Dublin 2

Trade enquiries to CMD DISTRIBUTION,
55a Spruce Avenue, Stillorgan Industrial Park, Blackrock, Dublin

Published in the US and Canada by the
IRISH AMERICAN BOOK COMPANY
6309 Monarch Park Place, Niwot, Colorado, 80503
Tel: (303) 652 2710, (800) 452-7115
Fax: (303) 652 2689, (800) 401-9705

© Raymond Murray, 1998

ISBN 185635 223 4

10 9 8 7 6 5 4 3 2 1

TO SÉAMUS MAC AN TSAOIR

Printed in Ireland by Colour Books Ltd.

CONTENTS

CONTENTS

Introduction

INTRODUCTION

IN SEPTEMBER 1967 I WAS appointed curate in Armagh parish. Chaplaincies in the various institutions in the parish were shared among the priests and it fell to my lot to minister in Armagh Prison. At that time it was the sole prison for women in Northern Ireland. Prior to 1970 it never housed more than a dozen or so women at a time, prisoners mainly on charges of simple drunkenness, assault, theft, fraud, forgery, prostitution and murder. A few poor women flitted in and out regularly. They were well-known characters who were often glad to get a shelter and build up their health again. The staff was very good to them and acted more as carers than wardens. The prisoners did some laundry work and some general cleaning. They wore prison clothes, a polka dot blouse (green for sentenced, blue for remands), heavy serge brown skirt, coarse stockings and block shoes.

Indeed much of the prison was used as a closed borstal for young men. About 40 young men aged 17 to 20 years were kept there. They were usually young prisoners who had given trouble in the open borstal at Millisle, Co. Down. Depending on good behaviour they were returned to Millisle after three to six months. They also wore a uniform, a black military bomber jacket, dark trousers and slippers. The prison was staffed by male and female officers; generally speaking the men were in charge of the borstal boys and the women were in charge of the women prisoners.

If one walks down the beautiful mall in Armagh one will see the former prison at one apex, a fine classical building, now listed for preservation. It was built in 1780 and replaced a military barracks which had been constructed on the site in 1736. This building fronting the mall was the admittance section and administrative part of the prison. The cell wings lay to the back. The prison was Victorian in style inside. The stone-built cell wings at the rear dated to 1846. There were two main cell wings emanating from a circle, one two-storeyed (A Wing) and the other three-storeyed (B Wing). These wings held 140 cells. Admittance to the wings from the circle was through a double closure, a door and a gate. A prison officer was constantly on duty in the circle to lock and unlock doors and gates. In 1976 a small third cell block, known as C Wing, was opened in one of the prison yards. It was a two-storeyed concrete building with 30 cells.

After 1970 the number of prisoners began to increase when the political situation deteriorated into civil strife and then war. The main male prison, Crumlin Road, Belfast, was grossly overcrowded in 1971 and Armagh Prison was then used to house 132 men. These men were among those who had been arrested under Emergency Powers and tortured by Special Branch RUC and British soldiers in two main interrogation centres, Girdwood Park Barracks, Belfast, and the Palace Barracks, Holywood, centre of the Parachute Regiments. Fr Denis Faul and I published a pamphlet on this ill-treatment in 1972, *British Army and Special Branch*

RUC Brutalities, December 1971– February 1972. By 1971 over 1% of the Catholic male adult population in Northern Ireland had been imprisoned or interned and over 2% had been arrested and interrogated. The whole nature of the prison changed. The vast majority of the new prisoners had been severely tortured and on the basis of forced confessions had been charged with serious offences like arson, shooting and bombing. I saw myself the many bruises and injuries on the prisoners' bodies that had been inflicted on them during the police interrogation procedures. The prison became a top security institution, guarded by soldiers with arms at the ready, barbed wire and military observation posts.

Brutality and ill-treatment in some police stations and in the two major interrogation centres, Castlereagh, Belfast, and Gough Barracks, Armagh, continued until 1979. In 1976 the European Commission of Human Rights found the government of the United Kingdom guilty of torture against detainees and in 1978 the European Court of Human Rights found it guilty of inhuman and degrading treatment. Two Amnesty International reports on Northern Ireland, 1972 and 1978, also substantiated the facts of ill-treatment in interrogation centres. Prisoners were often jailed for long terms on the basis of forced confessions. A later new phase of violations of human rights emerged in the use of informers in the special one judge, no jury, Diplock Courts. People were often jailed on the uncorroborated evidence of informers of dubious character.

In August 1972 these male prisoners in Armagh were transferred to a new prison camp, then called Long Kesh, later known as the Maze Prison.

In Armagh Prison the number of women political prisoners increased from 2 in 1971 to more than 100 in the 1972–76 period. Thirty-two of these women were imprisoned without trial. Most of the women political prisoners were girls in their teenage years but one internee was in her sixties. The first of the women internees was Elizabeth McKee who was interned by the secretary of state, Mr William Whitelaw, on 1 January 1973. In the 1972–76 period the prisoners had Special Category or 'Political' status. The establishment of Special Category status benefited indirectly all prisoners. It meant the growth of educational facilities and all women prisoners in Armagh were allowed to wear their own clothes.

In the 1974–76 period the problems of those concerned for the welfare of prisoners were threefold:

1. Legal – to establish the innocence of many who were behind bars without trial or without a fair trial. Discrimination against Catholics still existed, despite Westminster control over law and order, (a) at the level of arrest, prosecution and preferring of charges, (b) at the level of the operation of the courts.

2. The problem of ensuring that persons arrested were given humanitarian treatment in accordance with

international standards. Brutalities in interrogation centres and police stations and punitive sorties by soldiers in Long Kesh Camp continued despite major allegations of torture brought by the Irish government against the government of the United Kingdom in 1971.

3. To see that prisoners and their families were able to live a normal life free from harassment and financial ruin.

IN 1977 THE WOMEN POLITICAL prisoners joined the protest of the men political prisoners in Long Kesh against the removal of political status from all prisoners sentenced after March 1976. Unlike the men, the women were allowed to continue to wear their own clothes. However they lost many 'privileges' and 'rights' and were locked up for most of the day. This was a punishment for not working.

Due to the long sentences, ranging from five years to life imprisonment, and the confined nature of imprisonment due to continual lock-up in their cells, many prisoners contracted illness, seven of them suffering from anorexia nervosa. They had little fresh air and there was no greenery. The prison yards were very small and outdoor recreation was drastically curtailed.

On 19 April 1979 a great tragedy occurred. A woman prison officer, Mrs Agnes Wallace, was killed and three others were wounded in a gun and grenade attack outside the prison.

Due to protests in the prisons against the imposition of work and a ruling to wear prison clothes, and against the punishments inflicted for refusal, alienation of the prisoners from the authorities increased. More and more international bodies and human rights movements criticised the British government for the interrogation procedures, ill-treatment of prisoners and injustice in the courts.

The whole social background to the prison problems was one of poverty, deprivation, mass unemployment, internment, harassment by police and soldiers, repeated arrests and long detentions incommunicado. These were all part of the grievances of prisoners, their families and their communities.

A very serious situation arose in Armagh Prison on 7 February 1980. There were serious allegations from the women that they were beaten by male officers. They then escalated their 'no work' protest to follow the example of the men in the H Blocks, Long Kesh, in the 'No wash' 'No slop-out' protest. They were then locked up 23 hours a day in their cells. The soiled cells were left dirty for the first six months.

The hunger strike of the men in the H Blocks lasted 217 days. Ten of them died. Three women had joined the first hunger strike. Their fast lasted three weeks and ended with the discontinuance of the first hunger strike.

In the post hunger strike situation, although much was recovered by the prisoners, the British government lost an opportunity for reconciliation with the Catholic community in failing to be generous in the settlement terms. Only 50% of lost remission was restored, which meant that some prisoners on long sentences served extra years.

From 9 November 1982 the Northern Ireland Office under Mr James Prior, MP, and later Mr Nicholas Scott, MP, initiated the policy of stripping the women prisoners naked. All women prisoners entering or leaving prison for whatever reason, on parole, visiting a hospital, on remand in the courts, at trials, were stripped naked and visually examined back and front. This caused the prisoners great suffering.

My prison reports reflect the problems in Armagh Prison. They are to be gauged against the changing moods and emotions in the prisons and in the community from 1970. A good spirit and good relationships within the prison varied according to official policies pursued and the enlightenment, or lack of it, of successive authorities. Problems in the jails spilled over into the community. Events in other prisons and in the community at large had effects on prison life. It is clear that internment and the removal of Special Category status were major mistakes. There was no feeling on the part of government to bring peace through a policy of understanding and generosity. Institutional violence inevitably helped to escalate resistance in Northern Ireland and prolonged the war. The government and the Northern Ireland Office turned a deaf ear to concerned community leaders who advised a softer policy in the prisons. This was frustrating. One can notice that my reports became more hard-hitting as injustices increased and oppression grew.

Two former women prisoners in Armagh Gaol were killed. Mrs Máire Drum was murdered by the UVF on 28 October 1976 in the Mater Hospital, Belfast, where she was a patient. Mairéad Farrell, along with companions, Daniel McCann and Seán Savage, unarmed members of an IRA active service unit, were shot down by the SAS in Gibraltar on 6 March 1988. The European Court of Human Rights, 27 September 1995, found that the three had been unlawfully killed, that the British government was guilty of having breached Article 2 of the European Convention on Human Rights, the Right to Life.

In March 1986 the women prisoners were transferred to Maghaberry Prison in the diocese of Down and Connor and so my chaplaincy ceased.

ARMAGH GAOL
Extracts from Catholic Chaplain's Reports

1971: ARRIVAL OF MEN POLITICAL PRISONERS

ON 10 JANUARY 1972 I received the following statistics from the office in Armagh Prison:

Male Prisoners: Number of sentenced prisoners	32
Number of Catholic sentenced prisoners	2
Number of prisoners on remand	77
Number of Catholic prisoners on remand	64
Female Prisoners: Number of sentenced prisoners	14
Number of sentenced prisoners – Catholics	8
Number of prisoners on remand	2
Number of Catholic prisoners on remand	2

This generally is in keeping with the overall picture of this 'province' where over 1% of the Catholic adult male population has been imprisoned or interned, and in fact over 2% has been arrested and interrogated.

The vast majority of prisoners in Armagh at present are on remand for charges of a political character. This has led to certain new problems of a serious nature for the prison chaplain. The ordinary prisoner on a criminal charge, whom we would hope would find himself in an environment compatible with a speedy rehabilitation, now finds himself in a top security prison guarded by soldiers with arms at the ready, barbed wire and military observation posts. Open space has been drastically curtailed in the prison. This and the overcrowding has made impossible the therapeutic values of occupational work and recreation. Where the mental resources are slight but where physical energies are considerable, prisoners have little outlet for their energy and feel a cabin fever. Educational facilities are practically nil. Prisoners were deprived of one of the chief means of occupying themselves when the authorities banned the admission of felt pens.[1]

The closing of Castledillon Open Prison was a severe blow to the ordinary prisoner (non-political). It was a new experiment and a successful one. The ordinary prisoners feel that they should not be in jail in Armagh Prison in its present form.

Visits are short and cannot be divided. Prisoners, particularly married people, object to visits in the presence of a prison officer.

Because of all these factors mentioned, it is difficult to keep up the morale of prisoners.

Women Prisoners
Due to present circumstances women prisoners find themselves very short of space and facilities. Married women prisoners should have two visits a month, if not every week.

16

This is essential for spiritual and mental equilibrium. The sight of their married partner gives them confidence and renews their fidelity. Again, I say, a certain degree of privacy is desirable for married people during their visits.

One notices a particular set of female prisoners coming in again and again from Derry city. In a large city this type of person would be absorbed in the subculture of the city. They would be tolerated and confined to this subculture. Generally it would be welfare people who would assume charge of them from an early age. The danger of a small city is that these people would come into contact with the police first and then would remain a continual problem of the police. I expect to see them continually return to prison until their way of life finally destroys their health. It is not too much to say that their mental health stability is very poor and most of them have been in mental hospitals.

Prisoners on Remand
Continual remands in custody means that many of these men are in a state of anxiety and uncertainty. Many of them arrive in prison with serious bruises on their bodies as a result of police interrogation. One man, Joseph Rafferty, had to be removed to the Musgrave Hospital for seven days from Armagh Prison. In my opinion severe mental damage has been done to many of these men due to interrogation with brutality. Modern penological methods regard the necessity of a psychological examination as a matter of routine for people entering prison. Where there is evidence

of stress, as there is in many of these cases, it is imperative.

The vast majority of the remand prisoners are from Belfast and come from the poorer section of society. Visits present special difficulties for the relatives. Almost all have to come on the bus and the fare is £1.25. A trip to Armagh is a big expense to pay for a mere 15 minutes visit. The minimum should be 30 minutes.

The Law

Prisoners are very interested in the operation of the law. Often they regard their own sentences as harsh in comparison with others whose cases seem to be similar but whose sentence was of lesser severity or was suspended. The danger is that they will brood over their treatment and regard it, rightly or wrongly, as unfair. They need to have their legal rights as prisoners, whether on remand or later as convicted prisoners, explained to them. Whether that is to be done by the visits of their own solicitors or by a simple educational programme is not for me to say.

Internment

Since the great majority of the prisoners on remand are Catholics, when internment took place they shared in the general fear that spread through the Catholic community outside on hearing that the protection of law had been removed, as they concluded, from the Catholic community. Prisoners are very vulnerable in ordinary times but Catholic prisoners feel they have little protection inside prison, and they stand in danger of being interned or detained on leaving the prison. In fact this has happened to some Catholic prisoners, one of whom is in a mental hospital. Indignation and sympathy combined, on account of internment, led to a hunger strike.

Special Cases

It was prudent and praiseworthy that when Armagh became an adult prison, and later a high security prison, that the borstal boys were removed from the prison. The conditions of change and its added tensions would have had ill effects on borstal boys. It is disturbing that prisoners of 16 and 17 years should be on remand there at present. A disturbing and imprudent incident occurred in early January 1972 when a young boy under 14 years of age was securely lodged in the prison. After a week he is still here at the time of writing. It is difficult to surmise the damage that could be done to this child by this experience. I might add that his mother died a few years ago and only his father and two brothers are at home. This incident has led to a lot of talk among the prisoners.

Recently I broke the news to a female prisoner, and on another occasion to a young male prisoner, that their fathers had died. It was pitiful that they could not attend the funerals.

Rehabilitation

Is sufficient being done for the prisoners to prepare them

for leaving the prison which is a traumatic experience? I think they would need to have a special interest taken in them for a month before and several months after leaving prison. One would welcome a conference of all profess-ional people who have to do with the rehabilitation of pris-oners: welfare workers, sociologists, chaplains, doctors, and psychiatrists. A news-sheet of local penology for the 'pro-vince' would be very welcome.

1972: Torture and Ill-treatment in Interrogation Centres

Torture is the frightening word which comes to a chaplain's mind recalling the first months of 1972 in Armagh Prison, when remand prisoners were admitted still bearing the marks of psychological and physical brutalities they had been subjected to. This was the period when Catholic detainees were taken to the RUC interrogation centres in Holywood and Girdwood Barracks and torture used to force them to sign statements admitting crimes that the police wanted to connect them with. The men were then charged on the basis of torture statements. Some of these men were on remand in Armagh Prison where I met them and saw the marks on their bodies. It is fair to say that all those who had to do with the detention centres where the detainees were ill-treated are dishonoured by what happened, not only those who actually inflicted the brutalities, but also senior army and senior police officers who allowed it to happen. The conduct of the army doctors was unethical.

It was a relief when Mr William Whitelaw came to Northern Ireland as Minister of State. Guarantees were given that brutalities in army barracks and police stations would cease. The effects on the Catholic population have been catastrophic. Their confidence in the law was undermined when men in charge of the law so violently broke it.

By the time Mr Whitelaw came on the scene the brutalities were accepted as the truth. Too many detainees had been ill-treated to hide it from their relatives, doctors, solicitors, and priests. Minute dossiers had been compiled by prominent church and medical men. Their aim was a short-term one – to stop the ill-treatment of prisoners immediately. The *Sunday Times* presented a most telling report. International conferences in America and Germany discussed the problem of torture in Northern Ireland. As late as 8–11 October 1972, it was a subject discussed at the reunion of the International Commission of Prison Chaplains in Rome. The long-term message that this must never happen in the United Kingdom came across in a special programme by the ITV *World in Action* team. That programme, *A Question of Torture*, will remain as a valuable historical documentary. The story is also preserved in medical journals.

The weight and wealth of medical and hospital evidence concerning the brutalities was so great that it could no longer be ignored. Despite the Compton Report and the British government's rejection of certain methods of interrogation, it was evident that there was still something seriously wrong with British army and RUC methods of interrogation. There was the disquieting consistency of statements, independent and free from collusion, that electric shock torture methods were used. When a break-through came, High Court judges held that torture confessions were inadmissible as evidence. Many major cases began to collapse because the crown at the last minute gave notice that it did not intend to use the suspect's confession, or the judge ruled that the confession was possibly not obtained voluntarily. A question that must be asked now – were any men already sentenced on the basis of torture statements before this apparent consensus of judges? Could this be reviewed and, if it did happen in some cases, what could be done for those individuals?

Even today there is some allegation of ill-treatment of men in custody in some police stations. The case of Gerald Donnelly, Gerald Bradley, and Edward Duffy shocked my colleague Fr Patrick McDonnell when he saw them after they were admitted to Armagh Prison. Thomas Kearns and John Kelly alleged they were given drugs in Newry police station. There was medical evidence. Was this accepted in court?

Northern Ireland has now a major prison world, not only because of the huge numbers imprisoned in Crumlin Road, Magilligan, Long Kesh and Armagh but in the last few years so many others have also passed through by internment, remand and detention; there is the world of the relatives and friends of prisoners; there is the world of those who have tried to feed and clothe their dependents. One senses the interplay between all these prisons and the condition of the country. For instance, a special Mass for peace was requested by the prisoners after the massacre of the 13 Derry citizens. Conditions and happenings in other prisons are major talking points. All this affects morale. Long Kesh is a major talking point among Catholics, not only for those in prison but for those outside – its huge size and cruel aspect, the growing military control there, the presence of Young Prisoner Category, stories such as those connected with John Carlin, Cyril Canning, and Compound 6 on 22 September 1972.[2] The International Red Cross in various reports has emphasised the physical and mental suffering of internment. The suffering is also felt throughout the Catholic community. The decision to continue with internment fills them with despair.

I mention two incidents in connection with the male adult prisoners who were in Armagh Prison until August 1972. January 1972 saw the imprisonment of a 13 year-old boy in an adult male wing. To the prisoners, to me, and to others in the United Kingdom, this contrasted with the Timothy Davey affair which almost weekly maintains pre-eminence in English papers.[3]

The other incident is the attempted escape by some male prisoners. One felt strongly the suffering of the two prison officers and the police officer who had been held captive. They were very brave. One would also pay tribute to the prison governor and staff who saw that the whole incident passed off without further repercussions in the period immediately afterwards.

Borstal Boys

The borstal boys came back to Armagh prison on 20 August 1972. One thinks immediately of the riot which occurred on their return. Happily it passed off without any serious injury. Their reason for rioting is baffling. Perhaps the change from their mood of independence in Magilligan to the strictures of borstal training was too sudden. Perhaps there is too much of a militaristic tinge in aspects of young prisoners' training which does not suit now, considering the political situation of the country. Perhaps they were influenced by the wave of unrest which was going on in English prisons at the same time. However the damage they did was untold. The whole affair was handled well by the governor. Punishment was not harsh and his enlightened policy paid off. Although there is always the danger of fluctuating sectarian feeling among the boys, at present it is slight and they have settled down well, although the authorities must always be wary. The boys are well-behaved in the religion class and services, and are as good if not better than those in the past. Depending on conduct and progress I think shorter terms should be given to borstal boys. I think it would be the best inducement if it could be coupled with proper arrangements for the continuing of their trade outside. The early life of these boys after they have left school amazes me. They seem to flit about a lot of menial jobs where they are paid scab wages. Apart from their family background and the social conditions of their living, it may be one of the reasons they get into trouble. Of course the breakdown of the state has had its effects, not only on these teenagers but also on infant children. It is sad to see such files accumulate on young people. I would suggest that when a person is released from prison or borstal that only the minimum statistics of their offences and medical reports be kept. A free person deserves a clean sheet as part of his human dignity. I think it would be a mistake to record that they are unionist or republican in their political views, or record their religious attendance prior to borstal.

Women Prisoners

There were few convicted female prisoners in Armagh Prison during the past year. I feel that they deserve a special place of their own, away from political prisoners.

1972 saw the gaining of special category 'political' status by some of the women prisoners. It has been granted and it should be carried out in a true and ungrudging fashion. I predicted this category last year. In a way it was self-evident, considering the state of the country. It is a pity that it was not done as an enlightened move without the approach of a hunger strike.

It is self-evident again that special category prisoners call for special trained officers. It calls for high qualifications in prison officers. This is only reality. Otherwise there could be mistakes. There is such pressure on the whole Catholic community that many now in all walks of life are emigrating. This could also happen Catholic prison officers and might affect the prisoners.

There are a number of things that seem to cause constant irritation among the women prisoners, especially those special category who are sentenced. One of these is the cooking of food, perhaps because they are women. They always seem aggrieved at the cooking. Could they not be supplied with a hot plate? It would also keep them busy. They would also like to have a tutor for Irish. They have already obtained permission for this. They would like a continuation of the practice of being locked up at 9pm and would not like this to be changed to 8.30pm. Occasionally they would like to see a complete film on television. They would like freedom in the choice of records and the design of handkerchiefs and leather work. They feel they should be on a parallel with Crumlin Road Prison in this. They regard half an hour outdoor exercise in the morning and afternoon as too little, especially in good weather.

The Law

The law, of course, is intimately connected with prisoners. They are intensely interested in it. They are intensely interested in the problem of an impartial police force and impartial courts. Special courts are not acceptable to the Catholic community. The British government has no standard regarding the extraction of statements by torture. If the Diplock proposals are accepted there will be further confusion. Britain should accept a universal standard such as is laid down in international law.

An argument is put forward that special court proceedings are necessary in Northern Ireland because of the intimidation of witnesses. Statistics prove that there is no need for Special Courts, or special laws for Special Courts. Recently statistics showed that there were about 278 convicted political prisoners and 215 on remand. That makes 493. Also about 250 are detained. What is the problem about intimidation of witnesses? The law is degraded by Special Courts. It throws the problem of peace and justice years ahead.

Two important concessions, I think, would add to prison reform. The first is parole. The Ministry of Home Affairs, Northern Ireland, has no statutory power to grant parole to prisoners in custody who are on remand or awaiting trial. Has anyone this power? If not, what does one do in the case of the death of a parent or child? Does it mean that a government which is to work for the common good would fail in what is an elementary charity? This one case, the death of a parent or child, should be reviewed in all categories of prison life in Northern Ireland. Considering that the individual has only one life, to be refused such a thing could have devastating effects on his future life. An argument against it is put forward – 'Consideration is given to conditions in the community'. If that argument be accepted, it could lead to all sorts of abuses against justice. It would create a 'Solzhenitsyn' world.

The other reform I am thinking of is special marital visits. Although our prisons have still got their physical Victorian look, surely penology should move out of Victorian views. I would ask the Ministry of Home Affairs to consult the churches, the departments of psychology in the universities and the various marriage guidance organisations on the subject. Such special marital visits of course would be confined to particular categories.

Finally, it can be said that imprisonment is one of the major social factors in Northern Ireland. I would suggest to the Ministry of Home Affairs to see that the universities undertake an immediate research project into prison life. I think, because of the many problems involved now in prison life and the 'prison world extension' outside, that such a social scientific inquiry is vital. In the meantime, of course, those involved in prison problems could help one another by the dissipation of knowledge of the problems and possible solutions.

1973: Enlightened Policy

Political Status

Armagh Prison is a very different place to the one I wrote about in my last two annual reports. Despite the many tragedies that are still happening in Northern Ireland, there is an evolving, though painful, change of attitude towards notions of equality and human rights. Many have been granted. The absence of others are publicly challenged. There are new top structures in government from whom at least there is hope of some redress. That was impossible in former Stormont days. Appeals then were useless. Now a new hope is seeping down through the community. This general situation is, I think, reflected in prison life. Since political status was granted, there has been a wonderful change, for example, in prison life in Armagh Prison. There is an enlightened governor and staff to whom the highest compliments and praise are due. I notice the prisoners have no longer the sense of vulnerability and insecurity which I wrote about in former reports. Patience, attention and kindness have paid off. There is hope for the future.

Parole

This is the most pressing problem, I think. It is here where the old 'situation in Northern Ireland' plea is devious. Whatever sliding scale is devised (who devises it and on what consultation?), the other side of the argument is better.

Compassion and charity have a better influence on human beings, and prisoners regard themselves as such. Whatever strict rules and regulations are laid down, there should always be enough room left to practise mercy and justice in extenuating circumstances. I think of married prisoners and prisoners who have relatives in other prisons (the present 'troubles' have hit families more than individuals).

The case of Brigid McMahon, where parole was due in justice, is an impossible one to understand. I had mentioned her special case in my report of 1971 when she did not get out for her father's funeral. If a government is for our good and service, a number of questions have to be answered here. Why was her parole turned down? Unless this is honestly and reasonably answered, then the only conclusion of a citizen of this state is that the whole pyramid of social workers, psychiatrists, doctors, prison staff, chaplain, and the work they have done in this case, is treated shabbily and shamefully. An explanation is essential.

Irish language tutor
There has been such a long delay in implementing this deep request by the women prisoners, and the knowledge that at least one able person of excellent character was passed over for the post, that one cannot help having the feeling that somewhere along the line there is a false identification of a cultural activity with extreme nationalism.

Women Prisoners

There have been only a few convicted women prisoners during the year. There has been little or no tension here, but I think they feel their situation more when they are in the same place as Special Category prisoners.

When I became Catholic prison chaplain here over six years ago, there were at the most six Catholic prisoners and sometimes none. Now there are about 70 Catholic women prisoners. They are not only symbolic but they do in fact represent a whole background of repression and suffering among the Catholic community which, one feels, is the result of political bungling. It also means they are a large enough group to be the object of the continual scrutiny of the Catholic community. We have seen in the past how even alleged ill-treatment of men in Long Kesh had disastrous effects in the disturbed areas of Belfast and led to the hijacking and burning of buses. This places a special heavy responsibility on people in charge of prisoners. Reports from other prisons in Northern Ireland fly around the whole prison world. It is quite clear that it was necessary to have independent enquiries into the deaths of Patrick Crawford and George Hyde in Long Kesh.[4]

Events outside have repercussions on the life of the prison world inside, especially events concerning other prisoners, such as ill-treatment by police, apparent injustice in courts, savage sentences, ill-treatment in prison camps. The forced feeding of the Price sisters is expositive of emotion in the prison world in Northern Ireland. One would feel a great sense of relief if these prisoners were brought over.[5] The prison world in Northern Ireland is aware that 18 prisoners have been transferred from prisons in Northern Ireland to serve their sentences in England – this information was given in a reply by Mr Van Straubensee to Mr Jock Stollard in the House of Commons. Problems of the law are serious in the prison world. Prisoners, like many of the Catholic community, believe that the courts are biased against Catholics in the granting of bail, in the length of the sentences and that the police are biased in preferring more serious charges against Catholics than Protestants. This is commonly believed by Catholics and they hold that it is brought out by statistics. One such study appeared in the past year: *Justice in Northern Ireland: a study in social confidence*, by Tom Hadden and Paddy Hillyard.

Internment of women

During the past year 12 women were interned. To work in a Catholic community is to realise the sense of injustice created and the intense dislike of the police this fosters. How? This 12 is balanced against the total number of loyalist prisoners interned (10) in Long Kesh, and this in spite of the assassination of 137 innocent Catholics, the blowing up of Catholic churches, schools, halls and parochial houses.

Facilities

The women prisoners would like more bathing and toilet facilities.

In all my six years I never found them more contented. I think early promotions, the good attention given them, the ending of the old 'militarism' marching, have brought about a wonderful transformation. They have none of the old bitterness. There is a chance for the good friendly qualities of working class boys to show themselves. Their background is the usual old story of broken homes, social conditions of low employment and unemployment; the destructive nature of the 'troubles' has added more. Catholic and Protestant boys do not easily mix freely in borstal, but there it is even better than outside. Ultimate blame must lie with those who have brought about the sectarian divide. One small thing – I think the old stereotyped punishment sheet should be re-worded. Some of the punishments in it are obsolete and read badly in private, not to say in public.

The boys are always extremely friendly and courteous in the religion evening session, not to speak of their respectable attendance at religious services.

It was heartsome to be invited by the Visiting Body of the Prison to accompany them on their round and listen to the proceedings of their meeting. Perhaps in the coming year this could go a step further when they might invite us to have a general discussion with them. Prison is such a big thing now that one would hope for a gathering of all people connected with prison life, ministry officials, sociologists, welfare workers, doctors, psychiatrists, prison officials, to prepare for the future so that a well-worked out

34

plan can be drawn up for rehabilitation when an amnesty is declared.

1974: Good Relations

Looking back on seven years as prison chaplain, I could say that 1974 gave hopes from a number of important angles. It was the first time I witnessed tolerant good relations between prisoners and staff, and that in a state of emergency. It augurs well for the future. I think a number of things helped towards this:

1. The excellent straightforward governorship of Mr Hugh Cunningham, Mr Hayes and Miss Simpson. I could say that all three were held in high esteem by staff and prisoners.
2. The Special Category status of political prisoners which allows for dignity and self-respect. Rumours that this would disappear under the Gardiner report can only have been circulated by people who have no experience of prisons.
3. Positive interest of the Board of Visitors, welfare authorities, and welfare members of voluntary organisations.
4. The splendid growth of educational facilities. Excellent. Again auguring well for new methods in penology.
5. Good sense, good relations, and good leadership among all groups of prisoners.

This high praise is not offset by the serious incident of 16 October 1974 when the governor and three members of the female staff were held hostage by republican and loyalist groups. The action had no bearing on relationship or conditions within Armagh Jail. It was due to the failure to inform the public of conditions in Long Kesh after the events there of 15–16 October 1974.[6] It is not off-set either, understanding the necessity of security, by the puzzling vetting by the RUC of Catholic artists for the Christmas prison concert.

Internment

Since 1 January 1973, 31 Catholic women have been imprisoned without trial in Northern Ireland. 18 of these are still jailed without trial, the right to a public and fair trial having been interfered with by the Diplock courts. Arbitrary imprisonment has been used against Catholics in every decade of the life of the Northern Ireland statelet. The Catholic community regards it as institutional violence. It was always their argument that peace means the safeguarding of personal values and the creation of a just society. The repercussions of the imprisonment of Catholic men, juveniles, and women, without trial is symptomatic of the failure of the powerful and the privileged to share. The procedures of the Long Kesh tribunals continued in 1974 to undermine confidence in the law.[7] Internees had no opportunity to test their guilt or innocence by normal judicial processes. Continual international interest in the Long

Kesh tribunals, and in particular hardship cases, exemplified the international dimension, an inevitable consequence since the 'Whitelaw Tribunals' violate Articles 5, 6, 7 and 15 of the European Convention on Human Rights. In 1974 there was a flashback to the 1971–72 period of Armagh Jail when Dr Cole, the prison doctor, and I were summoned to appear before the European Commission on Human Rights of the Council of Europe, Strasbourg, regarding the ill-treatment of prisoners.

Parole

I would regard this as a pressing problem. Following the work of the Protestant clergy at Feakle and the subsequent cease-fire, there is a new atmosphere in the prisons and community. There is an assumption that there will be an amnesty for all political offenders. The prison populations interpret the recent exercise of the royal prerogative of mercy to release 100 prisoners who had almost completed their sentences as a move towards general amnesty. The result is that many are now in a state of excitement and hope. It is plain that in the present situation as the tension eases in the community, it rises in the prisons due to expectation. It is specially noticeable among the compassionate cases – the married, those who have already served a number of years, those who have sick members in the family or who have been bereaved, families where a number are imprisoned, elder imprisoned members of families who are needed to maintain the home. I think that it is this type of sentenced prisoner who needs parole. Internees are expecting releases not parole. Parole in their case can sometimes aggravate.

The Law

The law, of course, is watched by prisoners. They read court cases avidly. Sections 5 and 6 of the Emergency Provisions Act 1973 come in for the greatest scorn, and this would be true of the reaction of many in the Northern Ireland community.

Legal history was made in the case of Mrs Bernadette O'Hagan who refused to recognise the court and had a sentence of two years imprisonment on her at the Belfast City Commission, on an arms charge, quashed by the Court of Criminal Appeal, 16 December 1974.

Great hardship was caused by Section 7 of the Emergency Provisions Act 1973. It was in this section that prisoners critically compared discrepancies and disproportions of sentences to different sections of the community.

Long delays in the hearing of cases, long remands, continue to build up bitterness against the law and give the courts a monster caricature.

Borstal Boys

I would say that there is a very good spirit among the borstal boys. There is less and less of the old style military training. Again the interest of the Board of Visitors is having good effects. But I think the caring attitude of the governor and staff has influenced the boys for good to a great extent. Promotion to Millisle, especially swift promotion based on good discernment, seems to have good results. Two allegations fairly quickly on top of one another tended to mar this happy picture. Emmanuel Fusco complained that on the night of 6–7 September 1974, while in a cell with Thomas McGuigan, James Burns, David Hans and Michael Belshaw, some of them were struck, stripped naked, and hit by three warders. On the second alleged event, Brian Gillen complained of being hit by warders on 20 November and 21 November. Both complainants alleged that they had been threatened not to tell the governor.

Meeting of International Commission of Prison Chaplains

The meeting of Commission Internationale Permanente des Aumoniers Généraux des Prisons took place in London 23–26 September 1974. This covered conditions in European prisons. A special session covered torture and internment in Northern Ireland. There was a long debate on the modern penal system, especially aspects of the reform and rehabilitation of the offender. Research has shown that prison is not the ideal place for reform and, of course, bad prison conditions make it impossible. The larger the institution and the longer the sentence the more questionable the atmosphere becomes. Long Kesh was picked out as an example of that. The chaplains agreed that the following postulates should be transformed into deeds:

1. The prisoner's human dignity must in no circumstances be violated.
2. The rights of the prisoner as an individual and his freedom may only be restricted to the extent that it is strictly necessary for the purpose of judicial examination and punishment.
3. Neither the state nor the community is absolved from obedience to the commandment to show Christian love towards the prisoner. It places on them the obligation to do everything possible to help the prisoner to make a fresh beginning and to rebuild his/her life.
4. In the treatment of the prisoner nothing should be done that offends against human dignity and the precept of love: there must be no unnecessary repression or brutal treatment. Everything is to be encouraged that will lead to the development of the personality and to spiritual and mental rehabilitation.

Conclusion

During the past year I have been accommodated to the full by the governors and staff regarding religious exercises and duties. They have been most helpful and courteous. I am grateful to them. I am pleased to say that Cardinal Conway, Bishop Daly of Derry, and Bishop Lenny visited the prison. It is hoped that 1975 will see progress towards hoped-for reconciliation, intensive dialogue and concrete

Christian collaboration. For Catholics it is a Holy Year when they are called to Repentance and Reconciliation. In Northern Ireland we have always suffered divisions and lately fratricidal war. Let us pray:

Man, even though he is not detained
is yet often a prisoner,
a prisoner of his own dream or delusion,
a prisoner through what he does
or does not do.

Man asks for liberation,
an open door to outside,
to hope, to future and happiness.

The gate, even though man has locked it
with bars of iron,
God can open again to the new light.

Freedom, granted also to others,
can give me the freedom again.

1975: THE FRUIT OF POLITICAL STATUS

IT IS A PLEASURE TO say that the fullest co-operation comes from the prison authorities in aiding a chaplain to carry out his spiritual duties in Armagh Prison. I have always been given help in requesting times of services, and when other priests wished to make spiritual visits, they, like myself, were treated with the utmost courtesy.

The number of women in jail is still very high when one thinks back to the odd few in pre-1969 days. The political upheaval is still reflected in the high prison population, many of them teenagers. I think it was a wise and enlightened step to transfer the young girls bordering on the 15–16 age group for training in St Joseph's Training School, Middletown. They were removed from a political atmosphere and I imagine they have done well and that reports have been good regarding their conduct and training. It was a pity that one remaining girl of that age group was not transferred also, even at a late stage.

Internment of Catholic women ended during 1975. In all 31 Catholic women were interned in the present emergency. It is hoped that this immoral step of the British government, an infringement of human rights, will not be used again for any of its citizens. Even on the practical prison side the internees had an upsetting effect on sentenced prisoners.

Generally speaking, I think the atmosphere among the women political prisoners in 1975 has been good, so also their relations with the staff. Life has fallen into a working routine; they keep themselves busy at crafts and domestic work and they have good education facilities. These have been built up over the past few years. I think also that the welfare workers and the nursing sister do a good job. It is my opinion that the present prison reforms were brought about through the granting of Special Category status. One hopes that imprudence in this matter will not wreck the present harmonious atmosphere. It is clear from the past six years that in vulnerable institutions like prisons a crisis will spill over into the wider community. Perhaps there should be further discussion and communication on the subject. The forum organised last year by NIACRO was an encouraging if pie-in-the-sky effort to bring all groups and individuals associated with prisons together.[8] Such a meeting, which would discuss present issues of penology in a strife-torn country, would be very welcome.

Borstal Boys

During 1975 the Boys Borstal Institution was wound up. It is a blessing in disguise. Even at the best of times it had a shameful and shabby look; young boys in blue denim gang-type clothes in prison cells; doing punishing soul-destroying jobs like scrubbing floors and breaking up scrap. It would be interesting to see statistics down the years as to the success rate of this type of training. How many of them landed back in prison? I think, however, that a whole re-volution in this regard is before us. The training schools are doing marvellous work and facilities in them are excellent. As problem children are trained at a young age, the closed type institution for the ordinary delinquent may not be necessary. What complicated the Borstal institution in 1975 was the mixing of a high number of boys associated with paramilitary groups with the rest of the boys. The proport-ion of these types was too strong. It does not have to be left to the imagination to understand the serious effect this would have on the general body. All this came to a head in two serious riots. During the previous twelve months there had been a number of serious allegations from boys of being beaten by a few officers. One of the major complaints they made to the chaplains at the time of the riots was their resentment of the punishing military style drilling in the prison yard. Apart from two young girls, one of whom was hysterical following the noise of the riot, there was little re-percussion in the women's wing.

Law

Two aspects of the law during the year came as a major shock. One was the sentencing of a woman on a first charge. There was clear evidence of psychiatric disturbance. For-tunately the sentence was rescinded. The other was a borstal boy who also suffered from a serious psychiatric ill-ness.

45

1976: Ending Political Status

AT THE OUTSET I WOULD like to express my grateful thanks to the governor and vice-governor of Armagh Prison who have facilitated me in every way in the pursuit of my spiritual duties. There has been every help regarding Mass times and other services and my colleagues and I have been treated with the utmost attention and kindness during visits.

Ending of Special Category Status for those sentenced after 1 March 1976

Due to the political atmosphere the number of women in prison is still high. Prior to the political convulsion in Ireland the numbers were minimal. It is likely that these high numbers of prisoners will continue, often involving teenagers, while the political situation remains sterile. The Special Category prisoners are slowly trickling out, having served their sentences. In my Report of 1975 I expressed the opinion that there was a good atmosphere between these prisoners and staff and hoped that the system would not change. Unfortunately it has; in my opinion there is a blindness towards the extraordinary situation that faces us in a crisis period. Now new political prisoners, 14 on remand, and 4 sentenced, will be denied these rights. It means that two sides will face each other as enemies in the future. It has already led to the deaths of innocent prison warders.

The ordinary citizen who follows events here can see this prison upset spilling into the community. I cannot understand how civil servants ride on the wounds of others.

The present position of the 4 sentenced for 'political' offences is extreme. They are locked up 8.30am until 11.45am, during dinner 12.30pm–1.20pm; 1.30pm–3.45pm, 4.30pm–5.30pm (tea lock-up), 8.30pm until morning. All this on weekdays. Saturdays and Sundays they are unlocked during the day except dinner time, but are locked 5.30pm until morning. Were you ever stuck in a lift for a few hours? Self-imposed or whatever, this long locking-up is torturous in the extreme. I cannot understand either why educational facilities are withdrawn as a form of punishment. This is a complete abandonment of the principle of rehabilitation. It may be in keeping with the crude Victorian prison but surely would be a cause of scandal among penologists outside Britain.

Law

Questions of law still occupy a major talking point among prisoners, their relatives, and those involved in social issues. One of these is the problem of duress, the holding of prisoners for 72 hours or 7 days, not admitting solicitor, doctor or relatives. Different political groupings in Ireland have maintained that this has led to the sentencing of some innocent parties. That has and will be an enormous crisis for the individuals and families concerned. It is enormously damaging to the law.

Nobody in the community can understand why the British army and RUC seem to be immune from prison sentences for offences, for killing people and assaulting prisoners.

As outside, it is common talk within prisons that there is serious disparity of sentences as between 'loyalists' and 'republicans'. It is also felt that this bias is shown in regard to parole when relatives are seriously ill, in refusing bail, and in the preferring of charges.

Star, i.e., non-political men prisoners
A small number of male 'star' prisoners are kept in Armagh Prison. Strangely enough the Catholic members are not happy. They feel they are part of the standard 'Catholic' allowance in the state (a third of everything) and that warders are too close to them – in Crumlin Road Prison they could get lost in the great numbers and be left alone to their private thoughts and worries. One in July alleged he was struck by an officer, another alleged verbal abuse from an officer.

Special Category Prisoners
There have been constant complaints from the Special Category prisoners of small things which they say add up to degrading treatment. One is what they describe as a kind of 'Chinese torture' on B2 and B3; this is the turning on of the lights in the cells every half hour during the night. This keeps some from sleeping and disturbs others. On B1 ap-

parently they can turn their lights down. They complain of the warders who tease the dogs and keep them barking during the night. They also complain of the banging of doors during the night and the banging of the gates and doors if warders are asked to attend to a sick person during the night.

Visit of loyalist paramilitary leaders to Long Kesh

The main cause of shock among those interested in prisons was the report in the newspapers, 31 March 1976, that the leader of the Ulster Defence Association, Andy Tyrie, had been given a guided tour of a new top security cell block being built in Long Kesh Prison. The UDA have committed many murders of Catholics and have publicly claimed them. It was reported that Tyrie was part of a four-man delegation from the Ulster Loyalist Co-ordinating Committee, the umbrella organisation embracing most loyalist paramilitary groups, and that they were shown round the cell block by prison governor Mr Stanley Hilditch. It was reported that a government spokesman confirmed the visit and said, 'They have not been shown anything more than a prisoner would see'. It was reported that John McKeague, a deputy chairman of ULCC, who was among the delegation, said that the visit was requested by his own organisation during a meeting held with Northern Ireland officials to discuss the ending of Special Category status. On 31 March 1976 it was again reported in the newspapers that the Northern Ireland Secretary, Merlyn Rees, said on

30 March 1976 that the visit of the Ulster Loyalist Central Co-ordinating Committee to the Maze Prison was in line with government policy to talk to as many bodies and individuals as possible and to explain arrangements for ending Special Category.

A simple question. What would the reaction of the British community in Northern Ireland have been if the leaders of the IRAs, IRSP and other such paramilitary groups were shown round the prison by the governor? The above visit was shattering. It is just another example of the callous ignoring of nationalist feeling in Northern Ireland.

Punishment

In the 1970s through television we are being presented with the great strides in penology in other countries. The basic principle in Britain is still to punish. It seems to be the only answer on all occasions to prison problems. There is no trust in self discipline, proper work and pay. The real change must take place in the political atmosphere outside the prisons.

1977: WIDER REPERCUSSIONS

I WOULD LIKE TO express my gratitude to the governor and the authorities of Armagh Prison for the full co-operation and help received in carrying out my spiritual duties. I speak also for the other priests of the parish who say Mass in Armagh Prison and the priests and nuns who have been accommodated with spiritual visits. They have been received with courtesy and kindness.

Increase in political prisoners
The most significant thing about Armagh prison in 1977 is the new high rise of prisoners remanded and convicted for political criminal offences. It reflects again the convulsive state of politics in the north of Ireland. One had hoped that, as the Special Category numbers gradually dwindled and internment of women ended, things would return to some kind of normality. Now the figures are rising again at an alarming rate. A feature also of the political/social aspect of the north is the great increase in the number of women interrogated under emergency powers, a disproportionate number of them, as observed by commentators, Catholic women and girls from east Belfast.

Prisoners are now lodged in three wings: Wing C which houses the Special Category political prisoners; Wing B which houses ordinary sentenced prisoners and some twenty prisoners on political protest, a number which is steadily growing; short termers, among them four protest prisoners, and remands are in A Wing.

Protest prisoners

This corresponds with the general picture in the north, some 250 men being on prison protest in Long Kesh, the Maze. This poses a problem for the public at large and is becoming increasingly serious. By summer 1978 there will probably be some 500 on prison protest, meaning that one in every 100 adult Catholics and a small percentage of women will be, as it is termed 'on the blanket'. Whatever happens in prisons has repercussions in the wider community. Public feeling will be focusing on this problem more and more.

Health

In this situation health of prisoners is a major factor. One can notice the growing complaints of prisoners in Armagh Prison regarding the scant time allotted to them for fresh air activity. They say they have no outdoor recreation in the evening period, and other periods are restricted for what they regard as inadequate reasons – a machine in the yard, inclement weather, long delays in waiting because of shortage of staff. In this aspect Armagh Jail compares unfavourably to other female prisons, even in England. There is no green, the yards are small, the yard for C Wing is utterly too small. It would seem that provision should be made for outdoor recreation.

The physical drawbacks of Armagh Prison mitigate against developing the humanity and talents of the prisoners. The new low small-celled cell block with its constant fluorescent lighting and tiny yard is a step back. There is a constant feeling among female prisoners that they should have more privacy as regards washing, the use of lighting, the opening and closing of the doors of their sleeping quarters, as for example in Holloway Prison. One would hope that the health of the prisoners does not deteriorate. The object of penology is to take into account the particular characteristics of the prisoner. The health of one prisoner, Monica Craig, has deteriorated badly and I have drawn the governor's attention to this during the year.

Ordinary prisoners

Two of the ordinary prisoners who are working say they have little time to pursue studies. After work they have their evening meal; they have to see to personal things like washing clothes; they have then little heart and sometimes are too tired to study before lock-up at 8.30pm. On account of this one of them has dropped out of the education course. It would be better if some time could be provided for them during the day.

Star prisoners

There was the same number of Catholic men prisoners as usual. They make little comment but it may be useful to add that they, like the other prisoners, have noticed since

the beginning of January a good improvement in the cooking of the prison food.

Punishment following shooting of prison officers
However, twice in 1977 the prison population in the north
was subjected to what they regarded as 'arbitrary punishment' by the Prison Officers Association following the
shooting of prison officers outside the confines of prisons.
Statutory rights and privileges were withdraw, including
remand visits, appeal visits, family visits, incoming and out-
going mail, food parcels. In Armagh Prison all prisoners
were locked up for three days. On 26 July 1977 I wrote to
the Rt Hon. Roy Mason, secretary of state, the governor of
Armagh Prison, and Bishop Francis Lenny relating my experience when I was denied access to the Wings by prison
officers. I insisted on my rights. I later got categorical con-
firmation that these were not the governor's orders. There
has been no adequate report from the Northern Ireland
Office as to the legality of the Prison Officers Association
withdrawing statutory rights and privileges on these tragic occasions.

Ill-treatment in interrogation centres
It is unfortunate that one has to return to remarks made in
the 1971 and 1972 annual reports when I drew attention to
remand prisoners admitted still carrying bruises which
they alleged they received in RUC interrogation centres. It
is disheartening to find women and girls coming into pris-

on with stories of psychological and physical pressures they were subjected to in Castlereagh Interrogation Centre. I brought the allegation of one girl to the attention of the governor and the Northern Ireland Office. She had multiple bruising. In December 1977 Amnesty International visited the north of Ireland to investigate such reports and in December also the leaders of the four main churches said they were 'disturbed that serious allegations are being made of ill-treatment of suspects and prisoners' and 'it is a basic responsibility of the forces of law and order to seek to protect not only the public as they go about their lawful business but also persons who may be in custody'.

Consequences of these allegations of brutality and duress are that some prisoners claim that they have signed statements under pressure admitting crimes of which they are innocent. One prisoner in Armagh Jail got a retrial in June 1977. Her sentence of 15 years was quashed but she spent 13 months in prison.

Archbishop Tomás Ó Fiaich, my new religious superior, visited the prison twice.

Socio-economic factors

It is hoped that 1978 will see a softening in attitudes all round. It was interesting to hear the secretary of state, Mr Roy Mason, speak of his sadness at the number of young people involved in the 'troubles'. Bishop Cahal Daly has lately pointed out that it is the poor section of the community which has suffered most. He said, 'Surely it should not pass without notice that the sector of the population which receives most attention and most severity from the security forces, the sector that provides most candidates for court sentences and for imprisonment, are the people from the small houses and in the little crowded and unlovely streets. Surely we must be prepared to ask objectively whether some security policies might be alienating these people or leaving them open to the propaganda of subversives. It is surely a matter of concern that security is seen by so many of these people as oppression. Whether they be Catholics or Protestants, the people most subject to security searches, house searches, and interrogations tend to be from similar socio-economic and educational background'.

Amnesty

Recently the Taoiseach, Mr Jack Lynch, has hinted at an amnesty for political prisoners. All this could be the beginnings of a better situation ahead.

1978: SICKNESS, REMANDS AND PROTESTERS

FIRST OF ALL I WOULD like to express my sincere thanks to the governors and authorities who have facilitated me so well in the carrying out of my spiritual duties. This is a view also expressed by the other priests of the parish and visiting nuns and priests.

Looking back on 1978 three main problems stand out:

1. Sickness
2. The Plight of Remand Prisoners
3. The Problem of the Protest Prisoners

Sickness

A feature of Armagh Prison in the past year has been the long lock-ups of the women. This creates a grave psychological problem. It is in my opinion inhuman and degrading. Defeminisation. Many of the girls have been sentenced to long sentences. This with the punishment lock-ups imposed on the protest prisoners by the British government creates a state of helplessness. This in my opinion, and I have heard it also expressed by welfare and education officers to the Commission of Enquiry on Prison Officers Conditions, leads to a deterioration in the health of the girls.

In the past year we were faced with the serious decline in the health of three girls – Monica Craig, Patricia Mulvenna, Lorraine Halpenny.

Monica Craig suffered from anorexia nervosa. Her weight fell to five stones or thereabouts. One always had the fear that she would, in her critical condition, develop a chest infection, and die. Her case, which was deliberately kept from the public by those who were concerned about her life, at the same time attracted world-wide attention diplomatically, including the late Pope Paul VI, the British Prime Minister James Callaghan, MP, and the Taoiseach of the Irish Republic, Mr Jack Lynch, TD. She was visited in Armagh Jail by Archbishop Tomás Ó Fiaich, Armagh, and Bishop Edward Daly, Derry. Finally the Royal Prerogative of Mercy was exercised in her case. She was removed to an outside hospital. It is hoped that she will make a good recovery.

Patricia Mulvenna has also suffered a serious deterioration in health. It is hoped that no energies will be spared to get consultants and specialists to see her and keep her case constantly under review. In this respect also the anxiety of her relatives should be taken into account.

The illness of Lorraine Halpenny has also been a frightening experience. One noticed how withdrawn she had become. Harsh conditions for a long-term prisoner like her inevitably take their toll.

The situation of the long lock-up punishment for long-term protesting prisoners should be reconsidered. One would like to see the appointment of a psychiatrist to the prison to monitor the present effects and submit a report.

The Plight of Remand Prisoners

Due to the inadequate attention in the north of Ireland to matters of justice, prisoners on political scheduled offences remain for long periods in prison awaiting trial, quite often from a year to a year and a half. In other countries the judicial innocence of prisoners awaiting trial is presumed until they are found guilty by court. Britain herself through her foreign office, diplomatic corps, press, expresses high anger at the lengthy detention of her subjects charged for offences abroad – for example, young Britons on drug-trafficking charges. But as regards the north of Ireland, since 1968, one gets the impression that this humanitarian attitude does not apply. Consider the grievances of prisoners and relatives when the girl charged walks free from court having served the equivalent of a two or three year prison sentence. And there is no redress for this.

Following minor incidents in Armagh Jail in April, the remand prisoners on political scheduled offences were subjected to extremely long lock-ups for almost 24 hours a day. It is my opinion and the opinion of others that the continued attitude of long lock-ups for the remands is unjust.

The Problem of the Protest Prisoners

At present 37 girls in Armagh Prison and 363 men in the H Blocks of Long Kesh Prison, the Maze, are on protest for political status. The problem of prisoners in the north of Ireland is the problem of peace. There are approximately 2,000 republican or Catholic prisoners and 800 loyalist or

Protestant prisoners, using these words as loose descript-
ions. The problem includes all their relatives and friends,
numbering some 60,000, and now also, following the punishments inflicted on the prisoners on strike by the British
government, includes large sections of the communities in
Ireland and in the British Isles. The attention of the public
has been drawn dramatically recently to this problem by
two television programmes on BBC, one on ITV, and one
on RTE, not to mention the numerous news items on radio
and in the press. The argument for political status aside
(e.g., these people were sentenced by special courts having
been interrogated by special methods under detention by
emergency special laws and sentenced to special long sentences), the punishments the British have inflicted against
the strikers – taken together and inflicted on the prisoners
for over two years – constitute torture, degrading treatment, and are contrary to human rights. In the case of the
men: 24 hour lock-up, deprivation of physical exercise and
fresh air, no radio, no television, no reading materials, no
writing materials, no hobbies, no games, all lack of contact
with the outside world, no association with fellow prisoners, loss of all remission – and in the case of the women:
excessive lock-ups, loss of remission, weekly food parcels,
and film shows.

On 30 July 1978 Archbishop Tomás Ó Fiaich visited the
H Blocks in Long Kesh; he also visited Armagh Jail last
year on a few occasions. In his statement issued 1 August
1978 he had this to say, among other things:

The fact that a man refuses to wear prison uniform or to do prison work should not entail the loss of physical exercise, association with his fellow-prisoners or contact with the world outside. These are basic human needs for physical and mental health, not privileges to be granted or withheld as rewards or punishments. To deprive anyone of them over a long period – irrespective of what led to deprivation in the first place – is surely a grave injustice and cannot be justified in any circumstances. The human dignity of every prisoner must be respected, regardless of what crime he has been charged with. I would make the same plea on behalf of loyalist prisoners, but since I was not permitted to speak to any of them, despite a request to do so, I cannot say for certain what their present condition is ...

Several prisoners complained to me of beatings, of verbal abuse, of additional punishments (in cold cells without even a mattress) for making complaints and of degrading searches carried out on the most intimate parts of their naked bodies. Of course, I have no way of verifying these allegations, but they were numerous ... The authorities refuse to admit that these prisoners are in a different category from the ordinary, yet everything about their trials and family background indicates that they are different. They were sentenced by special courts without juries. The vast majority were convicted on allegedly voluntary confessions obtained in circumstances which are now placed under grave suspicion by the recent report of Amnesty International. Many are youthful and come from families which had never been in trouble with the law, though they lived in areas which suffered discrimination in housing and jobs. How can one explain the jump in the prison population of Northern Ireland from 500 to 3,000 unless a new type of prisoner had emerged?

The problem of these prisoners is one of the great obstacles to peace in our community. As long as it continues it will be a potent cause of resentment in the prisoners themselves, breeding frustration among the relatives and friends and leading to bitterness between the prisoners and the prison staff. It is only sowing the seeds of future conflict.

Pending the full resolution of the deadlock, I feel it essential to urge that everything required by the normal man to maintain his physical and mental health and to live a life which is tolerably human should be restored to these prisoners without delay.

The archbishop touched on the bitterness between the prisoners and the prison staff. Unfortunately I have to report that this has been a feature of the life of Armagh Jail in 1978 and I have told this to Mr Justice May's commission of enquiry into the conditions of prison officers. I am at a loss to understand what appears to me to be the callous indifference of the British authorities to these problems. At least six prison officers have been murdered, a prison official and a deputy prison governor. One can imagine what the feelings of the prison officers are to this? They have, however, taken the law into their own hands by locking up the prisoners and denying parcels and visits. For example, this was the action of the prison officers in Armagh Jail, 14–16 December 1978. Do the authorities realise the bitterness this causes among the prisoners who are so vulnerable? This combined with deprivations imposed on prisoners by prison officer industrial action, with what seems to the prisoners as a new 'get-tough' attitude on the part of the prison authorities in Armagh 1978, and the continued delay in restoring Special Category, keeps the frustration going, leads to bitterness and murder. One gets the impression that the British authorities are paralysed for an answer or are indifferent.

It is a good question. Do the British want a solution now? The necessities for physical and mental welfare are being denied to the prisoners. The vast majority of sentenced prisoners in Armagh are 'republican', 'Catholics' and they are on protest – 37. It is easy to see that education facilities cannot even function there. Prisoners suffer in health. Physical games facilities are almost nil. Relatives are going through anguish and suffering. I think it is the solemn duty of the British government, after 30 months of violations of human rights against the H Blocks and the protest girls in Armagh, to make moves towards a solution, to call in mediators, be they churchmen or statesmen, to allow the prisoners more contact with the outside world. The British government must make the first move, remove the excessive punishments which were designed to break the strike at an early stage and which have failed.

I would like to draw the attention of the British government to a report entitled *The Report of the Advisory Council on the Penal System on the Regime for Long-term Prisoners in Conditions of Maximum Security*, HMSO 1968 s.o. Code 34–455. The fact that it was published in 1968 before these 'Irish' problems should not mean that it be shelved ...

Things are difficult for officers and prisoners in Armagh Jail because the prison has really been divided into four prisons. There is really no need for this. In the present warlike situation in the north of Ireland, most of the girls committed to prison in the last ten years come from the same deprived and depressed areas – the Catholic ghettoes of Belfast, Derry, South Derry. They have much in common and it would be easier to deal with them together. The removal of political status has been the main cause of this. Things go smoothly in the wing of the Special Category and it is only there that humanitarian imprisonment can function – personal initiative, education, dignity. It must also be very difficult on prison officers to function in the other wings, their role being confined to that of warders. In former times relations were not so strained, even when the situation outside was worse and even when there were occasional crises in the prisons. The sadness of the present situation of prison officers was expressed by an officer on television lately:

> They could try and give them back Special Category Prison, Prisons, try and give them back for a short time, but there again I don't know if I am qualified enough to have that sort of thought, there again I am not supposed to think very much; I am supposed to know one particular job and do it.
>
> *How many officers would share your views?*
>
> I would say quite a lot, if they all thought about it anyway, because whenever people had Special Category you had all belonging to them, whether they were Provisional IRA or Loyalist. You moved among them. You could have a laugh with them. You could talk with them. If they wanted an aspro, you would get it for them. You'd talk about football; you would talk about dart matches, where they lived; you'd talk about their girlfriends, their wives and their kids. If they'd any problems at all they'd come to you if it was serious enough. It was your job and that's

what the whole job is, help them, help them.

It is so difficult now in Armagh Prison without the Special Category and with the new strained relations added to the fact that prisoners and prison officers are drawn from different religions, backgrounds, politics, culture – in fact the cultural divide is similar to that in the community outside.

A pathetic case
There are few ordinary prisoners. But there is one which causes great concern and I have written to the Northern Ireland office about it per Lord Melchett, namely the case of Miss ... , a sad pathetic case who is mentally deranged. She is continuously locked up, her detention in Armagh Jail is even a cause of scandal to all the prisoners. They pity her, and probably those with the mentality to send her to Armagh Jail. All say – 'she should not be there'. Surely there is some medical answer.

Star prisoners
Armagh Jail continues to have a number of male star prisoners. Of these the usual Catholic quota is four, reflecting the general quota of trust of Catholics by the government – as the prisoners themselves say. They continue to do the menial tasks, clean, maintain, cook, etc.

Hope?
One would hope that 1979 would see a break-through in

the very nasty situation which prevails in the prisons of Northern Ireland at present. Every means for the elimination of violence must be taken, but violent unjust institutional means are never justified or legitimate. To assume that security success and large prison populations under harsh conditions are a solution is part of the disease of the north of Ireland, where everything that happens is political.

1979: The Dignity of the Human Person

The year of Pope John Paul II

1979 might be called 'The Year of Pope John Paul II'. I think that many of the things he has to say have special relevance to the situation in the north of Ireland and especially the plight of the huge number of prisoners here. In his first encyclical, *Redemptor Hominis,* he spoke of the all-importance of the concrete, historical, live individual, the dignity of the human person, the person with a name. At the outset there is a lesson for all of us who deal with prisoners – do we give them a name or a number? Do we appear as upstart authorities taking advantage of their vulnerability, making endless play of minute things, calling them 'inmates'? 'All morality, Christianity and human rights, at least a person's commitment to these things, can be summed up in our attitude to this man or woman with a name – not some abstract man or woman'. Certain facets of the very strict regime mentioned in last year's report have been relaxed. I appreciate that the governor has exercised his discretionary powers in a compassionate manner in the last six months. However, the welcome improvement has been set back somewhat by the ultra-rigorous interpretation of rules in his absence. The denial of cigarettes to prisoners who have a right to them; the massive cell searches on Christmas holy night upset everybody and had a jarring effect on the spirit of Christmas; the body searching on Catholics going to Mass on the Sunday following Christmas.

The murder of Prison Officer Agnes Jean Wallace

The most tragic event of 1979 as far as Armagh Prison was concerned was the murder of Mrs Agnes Jean Wallace and the wounding of three other women officers. Fr Peter Kerr and I attended the funeral and were much moved by the poignant service. It is a terrible thing to report that 18 prison officers have been murdered since Special Category was removed. It is a terrible thing that we allow problems to be solved by violence and counter-violence. Last year in my report I quoted from Cardinal Ó Fiaich's address after his visit to H Blocks, Long Kesh, on 30 July 1978, 'The problem of these prisoners is one of the great obstacles to peace in our community. As long as it continues it will be a potent cause of resentment in the prisoners themselves, breeding frustration among the relatives and friends and leading to bitterness between the prisoners and the prison staff. It is only sowing the seed of future conflict.'

Protesting Prisoners

Has anything changed since then? Some 350 men are still suffering atrocious punishments in the H Blocks; the 24 women on protest in Armagh Jail, of course, do not suffer the same punishments which I believe over a period of time amounts to inhuman and degrading treatment. The situation should not be allowed to continue. It has lead to alienation, frightening alienation, in the prisons and in the nationalist community. The worst years of 1972–75 never saw such alienation as now exists in the prisons and this I have always said spreads into the community outside. It should not be allowed to continue, no matter how the men came to be in Long Kesh in the first place or the women in Armagh Jail; suspicion attaches itself to the interrogation procedures used at Castlereagh and other RUC interrogation centres which produced the statements that were accepted in surprisingly many cases by the one-judge, no-jury Diplock courts. 1979 saw the publication of the Bennett Report on this subject. It made several significant points: it cited the adverse findings of the European Court of Human Rights as proof of past ill-treatment of Irish prisoners (p. 50); detailed the fact that 'one of the constant features of the scene in recent years has been the large volume of complaints from prisoners about their treatment by CID officers during interrogation' (p. 52); which results in statements made by the prisoners implicating themselves and others in criminal activities which in turn results in the fact that 75%–85% of all convictions being based on self-incriminating statements. Unfortunately things have not improved – one now records weekly allegations of attempted blackmail and the most frightening thing of all, the acceptance by judges of so-called verbal statements, the most corrupt form of law.

The whole social background of poverty, deprivation and mass unemployment, of internment and British army harassment, repeated arrests and long detentions incommunicado, must also be considered as an essential part of the H Block scene and the women in the jail on scheduled offences. Add to this the grievance felt that no British soldier, no RUC detective has served a day in jail in Northern Ireland for killing or torturing persons while on duty in Northern Ireland and acting as agents of the British/unionist administration.

Besides his strong condemnation of violence of illegal groups, Pope John Paul II obviously referred to the British and Irish governments in a special paragraph which, it is clear, they choose to ignore:

> Every human being has inalienable rights that must be respected. Each human community – ethnic, historical, cultural or religious – has rights which must be respected. Peace is threatened every time one of these rights is violated. The moral law, guardian of human rights, protector of the dignity of man, cannot be set aside by any one person or group, or by the state itself, for any cause, not even for security or in the interests of law and order. The Law of God stands in judgement over all reasons of state. As long as injustices exist in any one of the areas that touch upon dignity of the human person, be it in the political, social or religious sphere, true peace will not exist. The causes of inequalities must be identified through a courageous and objective evaluation, and they must be eliminated so that every person can develop and grow in the full measure of his or her humanity.

The British handling of H Blocks blights peace. Will anybody in the Northern Ireland Office evaluate the problems of the protesting prisoners, will they remove the excessive punishments immediately? Will they seek mediation? Pope John Paul at Knock asked us to show people tempted towards the paths of violence another way of achieving justice and fair play. Those who possess power and authority and influence in Ireland should not earn for themselves titles of 'men of violence' but help show the other way. They should begin with the H Blocks situation and the problem of the protesting prisoners in Armagh.

Sickness

Long lock-ups and closed physical conditions must take their toll on health of prisoners. But more than anything long sentences. The sentences imposed in the courts of Northern Ireland are too long. It is ridiculous that any long-term prisoner should spend over nine years in jail. There should be a light at the end of the tunnel for every prisoner. Prisoners who at present are a source of worry are:– Pauline McLoughlin, Christine Sheerin, Marion Price, and Kathleen McIlviney.

Food

At present the prisoners say that the food is good. At other times they say it is of poor quality and badly cooked. There seems to be an adequate supply of nutritious food and good quality. The Northern Ireland Office has laid down rules for this. It is extraordinary then when there are occasions that prisoners complain of poor quality and bad cooking.

Remand prisoners

Prisoners are still waiting too long for their trial. This is an injustice in itself. Nine months is the maximum one could tolerate for awaiting trial.

Letters

It is absurd that prisoners are not allowed letters or cards from abroad on the whim that they do not know the people who are writing to them. Sounds like antediluvian penology.

Mass

In all my twelve tears as chaplain in Armagh Prison there was always the most courteous and helpful arrangements for Mass. It is sad that prisoners and their relatives have complained over a period of four months last year that the Catholic girls were prevented from going to Mass because of the practice of degrading body searches before Mass. They think this would not happen to Protestants going to their services. A special report was sent to the Vatican. The girls informed Cardinal Tomás Ó Fiaich of their situation following his visit at Christmas time.

It remains for me to thank all the prison staff who have helped me in my work as chaplain in 1979.

1980: ALIENATION

Black February

It is sad to contemplate that in the past decade so little has been learned by the British government in its treatment of Irish people. Anyone who watched the television play on ITV on 11 January 1981, *Playing for Time,* the grim story of a group of women in Auschwitz Concentration Camp, and had experience of Armagh Prison in 1980, could not but draw parallels at different levels between the two situations. In December of 1971 men were brought into Armagh Prison having been beaten in Holywood and Girdwood Barracks. Almost 10 years later, on 7 February 1980, now to go down in history as Black February, stories of the beating of the girls by male officers, the subsequent denial of access to the toilets, 7–12 February, denial of laundry and visits from concerned persons, and the 23 hour lockup, have been broadcast around the world. The girls, some 30 in number, have now been locked 23 hours a day for almost a year. Who in the wide world would inflict such a dreadful punishment on women? Do makeshift prison rules condone it? Does following the tradition of the founding of the concentration camps in South Africa by the British condone it? In the subsequent months in Armagh Prison the same human problem which came through in *Playing for Time* can be discerned in the numerous annoyances, hostilities, and hatreds that formed the picture of Armagh

Prison 1980 – anything to do with the Catholic religion, Irish nationalism were objects of violation.

Where and in what prison in the world today would a warder insist in opening the pyx which carries the sacred host when a chaplain brings a prisoner holy communion?

Should not pity replace the feeling of anger when energies are sapped scrutinising and confiscating records and books in Irish or to do with Irish history?

Racism and bigotry have to do with this human problem. It was a sad year for the priests in Armagh parish when on a number of occasions they were prevented from administering the sacraments of the eucharist, penance, and anointing of the sick in a dignified manner. This led to intervention by his eminence Cardinal Tomás Ó Fiaich and correspondence with the Northern Ireland Office. At present things seem to be resolved but the correspondence to the Northern Ireland Office shows that Catholic priests will not tolerate a lack of appreciation for the freedom and dignity and practice of their religion from a 95% staff not of their religion who are given bigoted leadership.

From 22–26 September 1980 I attended the International Permanent Commission of Catholic Chaplains in Lucerne, Switzerland, representing the north of Ireland where I made the following remarks about women prisoners:

> I feel that the Church has a special duty in the case of women prisoners for whom jail, even in reasonably relaxed and enlightened conditions, is a burden altogether unsuitable for them to bear even for a short period. I feel that the Church should campaign for the recognition of a

policy that women who offend against the laws of society would be kept in hospital-type institutions rather than be sent to prison cells. The Church has been challenged much of late in regard to its attitude to women. It has based its defence of its current policies very much on the psychology, mentality, and endurance between men and women. It must recognise that the longing for friendship and companionship makes women particularly unsuited for life in harsh prison conditions. A repressive and abusive system of confinement seems like hell to them. I regret to report to the assembly that certain aspects of the prison system for women in Northern Ireland come close to cruel confinement; I appeal to my fellow prison chaplains to take that same close interest in the case of individual prisoners and their rights and sufferings in my prison of Armagh as I have suggested to be the duty of the Church in every land.

Any institution of the state which destroys a person or diminishes him or her, or damages physical health, spirituality, or mental well-being, is an immoral institution and cannot be supported by the Church. All institutions of the state must prove their value to mankind by their ability to improve the lot of man. Many jail systems do not do this.

The serious illness of Marion Price and Pauline McLoughlin, who were released in 1980 when they were in danger of death, and the appalling condition of Dolours Price and Christine Sheerin are indicative of serious underlying problems in the Armagh Jail system. So also the condition of the protesting prisoners who have lost their remission (10 of them have completed their sentences and are doing 'overtime' – for instance Marie Doherty of Derry will soon have completed 4 years without remission). On 4 May 1980 parents of the protesting prisoners took the unprecedented step of meeting in Belfast and signed a statement which said:

> We are concerned that the dignity, spiritual rights, and
> self respect of the girls have been violated to a serious
> degree in Armagh Prison. We recognise that the means of
> protest available to our daughters were limited and that
> they were forced on to a 'no wash, no slop-out protest' by
> deliberate escalation of punishments which reached the
> final straw in physical beatings by men. This is not toler-
> able to Catholic people. All the members of the families of
> these girls have been personally insulted and injured by
> the cruel, inhuman and degrading attacks on their sisters
> and daughters. We find the actions of the British govern-
> ment and its agents deplorable but not unexpected after
> three years of a deteriorating regime in Armagh Prison.
>
> We support the five demands of the girls (1) vol-
> untary work, (2) free association, (3) free choice of re-
> creation and education, (4) one visit, letter, parcel per
> week, (5) restoration of full remission.

On the same day the parents replied to a letter sent to them
by Mr Michael Alison on 30 April 1980:

> The British administration under Mr Atkins and Mr
> Alison, and the senior officials of Armagh Prison, have
> lost all credibility in our eyes. We, the fathers, mothers,
> brothers and sisters of the Irish girls in 'A' Wing, Armagh
> Prison, feel that people who either organised, permitted
> or at least denied the beating of our girls on 7 February
> 1980 are unfitted for positions of public trust and we de-
> spise them. Protestant unionist warders were brought in
> to beat our sisters and daughters, 32 young girls beaten,
> manhandled and even partially stripped by men. This re-
> presents a new low in human misconduct. We cannot
> deal with the people who condoned this until the situ-
> ation has been rectified, the truth told, and those re-
> sponsible punished. To deprive the girls of toilets for five
> days, February 7–12, to lock them up 24 hours a day, no

hot water, laundry or sanitary towels during these days, to prevent their spiritual adviser and concerned people from seeing them for a week, these are other stupid and cruel abuses of power that we will not tolerate. To place men in charge of the corridors for five days February 7–12 with power to peep in through the peep holes at the girls locked inside and having to do their toilet in the cells, this is contrary to the decent Irish standard of modesty that we utterly reject in this British barbarism and savagery. Our reply to Mr Atkins and Mr Alison is NO, NO, NO.

1980 was overshadowed by the H Blocks protest, the protest in Armagh Jail, and the hunger strikes. On 27 October seven prisoners went on hunger strike in the H Blocks and three women in Armagh Jail on 1 December. The context was as follows: On 1 March 1976 Special Category status (political status) was removed from Irish persons as a result of the political conflict between Ireland and Great Britain by Westminster parliament. As a protest against this several hundred prisoners refused to do prison work and wear prison clothes (prison clothes have been abolished in many countries). They demanded voluntary work, free association, to wear their own clothes. The British answer was to impose excessive punishments which amount to torture, inhuman and degrading treatment contrary to Article 3 of the European Convention on Human Rights. These punishments were – complete removal of remission, 24 hour lock-up, deprivation of mental stimulation of any sort – reading material, television, radio, games, hobbies. This was combined with intimate body searches (protesting prisoners in Armagh Jail complained of intimate body searches in the toilet area going to and from visits, other prisoners complained of searches going to Mass, and visitors complained of body searches and hostility and sometimes hatred directed against them). In April 1978 the protesting prisoners in H Blocks went on a 'No wash' 'No slop-out' protest because they were beaten, they said, while performing these personal ablutions. The European Commission on Human Rights charged Britain with inflexibility on the H Blocks protests:

> the Commission must express its concern at the inflexible approach of the State authorities which is concerned more to punish offenders against prison discipline than to explore ways of resolving such a serious deadlock *(Report from Strasbourg, May 1980).*

There are signs now of a more flexible approach since the hunger strike gained world wide publicity. There are some indications as I write now 12 January 1981 of movement towards a solution. It is a shame that it took more than four years, a strong indication of political incompetence.

The legal system

A major study of the legal system in Northern Ireland by Mr Kevin Boyle, professor of law at the University College, Galway, Mr Thomas Hadden, lecturer in law at Queen's University, and Mr Paddy Hillyard, lecturer in social administration at the University of Bristol, outlined a series of criticisms of the judicial process and security policy in the north of Ireland. The authors said that more than half of the republican prisoners, whose trials they examined, were under 21 years of age – barely 11% more than 30 – while 43% had no previous record. Only 8% had previous convictions for 'ordinary' crime. 'They do not fit the stereotype of criminality which the authorities have from time to time attempted to attach to them'. They said that the remarkable low figures for political prisoners returning to active service contradicts assertions by some, including the Gardiner Committee of inquiry on the basis of whose 1975 findings Special Category status in prisons was withdrawn, that such status encouraged guerrilla activity. The report strongly urged the British government to allow all prisoners in Northern Ireland to wear their own clothes and to limit penalisation. The authors strongly criticised trial procedure in Northern Ireland, particularly with regard to 'confessions' – the circumstances in which they are obtained, the heavy reliance on them in securing convictions, and the absence of successful prosecution against police for alleged maltreatment.

One hopes that the alienation brought about by pressures on staff and prisoners will soon end. There is no reason why it should not. In 1970 I was writing in my annual report that the staff were a good emotional support to prisoners. It is sad that after ten years things plunged to concentration type conditions. In the past year alienation was at its highest. We must resist the notion put forward by British administration in Ireland that a convicted prisoner is entirely the property of the state. In particular we should resist any idea being accepted that the treatment of the mental and physical health of the prisoner should be entirely at the discretion of the agents of the state. In many prisons in Europe prisoners have access to outside doctors and their reports are available to them and to their families. There is no justification for the secrecy surrounding the health of prisoners in British jails. There was a break-through last year in the case of Pauline McLaughlin when an independent doctor was allowed to see her. The precedent has been set and now all sick prisoners must be entitled to this. It is important that provision would be made for independent professional men and women of the prisoner's own country and representatives of responsible international bodies and church agencies to have access to prisoners at regular intervals to ascertain that prisoners are in no way being destroyed, reduced, or damaged in their physical, mental and spiritual well being. This is the only way to face a regime of repression or neglect in any prison where prisoners suffer due to deliberate intent or to sheer carelessness or disinterest. Where prisoners are in a state of conflict with the agents of the state and they in a state of hostility towards them, there is a great need for independent professional people with access to prisons who will stand for the principle of human dignity and indicate the limits beyond which nobody should go, neither state nor individual, in their treatment of a fellow human being.

A chaplain may find persons entrusted to his charge who are being made lesser people by a system in prison, where their personality and health, physical and mental, are being destroyed by shapeless and ugly clothes, by mindless discipline, by meaningless work, by prolonged detention and overlong imprisonment. One thinks of Dolours Price and a few others who have no date of release. This is bestial in its cruelty for people who watch their daily sufferings and breakdown in health. She has served 8 years. She is not on a murder charge. And yet I have seen a prisoner released after 6 years in Armagh Jail, a non-political prisoner who was convicted for murder. The essential spark of hope, the human initiative, the development of responsibility and maturity may be deliberately inhibited. If a system does this, then it is an immoral system; it makes a person less a person. It destroys God-given qualities; the chaplain will have to fight against it, work against it with the weapons of the spirit.

1981: The Hunger Strike

1981 WILL PROBABLY BE LOOKED upon as a turning point in Irish history, similar to the executions following the Easter Rising of 1916. That led to the Anglo-Irish war. Sixty-four people were killed during the hunger strike, from 1 March on, more than half of them civilians. Seven people, two of them girls, aged 12 and 14, Carol Anne Kelly and Julia Livingstone, were killed by plastic bullets fired by the RUC or the British army. The deaths of the hunger strikers had of course serious repercussions in the jails.

The hunger strike lasted 217 days. The men who died were:–

BOBBY SANDS, MP, died on 5 May on the sixty-sixth day of his hunger strike.

FRANCIS HUGHES died on 12 May on the fifty-ninth day.

RAYMOND MCCREESH and PATSY O'HARA died on 21 May, both on the sixty-first day.

JOE MCDONNELL died on 8 July on the sixty-first day.

MARTIN HURSON died on 13 July on the forty-sixth day.

KEVIN LYNCH died on 1 August on the seventy-first day.

KIERAN DOHERTY, TD, died on 3 August on the seventy-third day.

THOMAS MCELWEE died on 8 August on the sixty-fifth day.

MICHAEL DEVINE died on 20 August on the sixtieth day.

The hunger strike is now over. Conditions have improved. Relationships between prisoners and staff have improved. Probably things will continue to improve under the softer and more enlightened regime of Mr Prior and Lord Gowrie. So then what was it all about and what was gained by anybody? In the beginning, of course, it was not about prison conditions. The British embarked on a policy of criminalisation, a foolish attempt to equate political prisoners with other prisoners. The international statistics of thousands of political prisoners must always be galling to tyrannical regimes, Ireland and Britain in the 1970s, Poland now in the 1980s, and the pattern is always the same: special powers, military oppression, and fear of the culture of the subjected people (the reason, of course, for forbidding Irish history books, Irish language dictionaries, and books in British jails!). Prison conditions did, of course, become a major factor when Roy Mason (where is he now?) imposed savage punishments for a minor strike, refusing to work and wear prison clothes. It is heartening to see at the present time that there is no going back by the authorities on this little man's savagery. He left Mrs Thatcher, Mr Atkins and Mr Alison with an unwelcome legacy. The matter, of course, could have been settled overnight (who does not believe that now?) but the Conservative government had to appear unbending in all its policies here as in Great Britain. So Mrs Thatcher did break the hunger strike. Conditions have improved, which proves my point that it was not about conditions in the first place. But who does not believe now that these political prisoners are different? In October I was on a lecture tour in the north of Italy. The children in the village knew about the hunger strike. Bobby Sands is a household name throughout the world. Mrs Thatcher has had a pyrrhic victory. She has ensured a military conflict here for another 10 years at least and did more than anybody to rouse the Irish in the United States.

The prisoners in Armagh Jail, of course, followed the story closely. They had endured severe punishments for a year. The story of their suffering will echo for many a long year. Will the British authorities not take a lesson not to base prison policies on punishment only even during emergencies? The compassionate policy should go on; remission should be restored in full; prisoners have suffered enough; there is no deterrent policy in serving double time, especially as the sentences in the north of Ireland are the severest in the world. GET THEM OUT! Statistics prove there is no return to violence on the part of the vast majority of political prisoners. There are few prisoners left in Armagh Jail. Moves should be made on releases, remission, prison activity, before the move to Maghaberry Prison. Education could start immediately – give them handicraft, Irish lessons, history, English and typing for a start. Shut down the Special Category – Christine Sheerin is in poor health – the whole history of her case is a legal freak – she should be released under licence. Pauline Derry, Etta Cowan, Christine Smith should be released also on licence – they have served long enough. The whole question of long-term prisoners has to be looked at NOW. Some years back the excuse was that long-term prisoners could not be released on account of the political situation and violence. How long then must they remain – until they are vegetables? Every person who has lived in the north of Ireland for the past 12 years knows that the political situation and violence is on-going – it does not take an intelligent person to know that the situation will continue for long years – boosted by Mrs Thatcher of course. So the problem of the long-term prisoner has to be faced. If 'review' has to mean anything, it must show there is reality and hope. If not, then there will be repercussions in the community – the prison world here spills out, not only at home but into Great Britain and the United States.

Prisoners are part of the promotion of justice. This is very easy to accept in Chile, Argentina, El Salvador, Poland, Russia. It is harder to accept at home because we understand all the complications. The complications then are an obstacle to justice. Then no action.

We should accept the challenge.

1982: POLITICAL FAILURES, PRISON FAILURES

We have then to find some form of torment which can give no sensual satisfaction to the tormentor, and which is hidden from public view. That is how imprisonment, being just a torment, became the normal penalty ...

GEORGE BERNARD SHAW

LOOKING BACK OVER MORE THAN fifteen years as a prison chaplain, and conscious of the affinity of prison life and the state of the country, it is sad to contemplate that the present 'war', now edged more with civil war aspects, has gone on for some twelve years; perhaps the longest sustained war in the proverbial seven hundred years of the Irish/English conflict, England's oldest and perhaps last colonial enterprise. It is astonishing for me to glance at the short little sentences of reports in the early days. But then I remember a time when there was not a single Catholic girl in prison in the north of Ireland. The situation of war changed all that. To flick through succeeding reports is to find the story of hundreds of young Catholic women, most of them well educated, many of them highly intelligent and talented, and all from the ghettoes. In another place and at another time they would hold high positions in society. Some of them who have gone abroad hold such high places. The interaction of the inside prison world and the outside community is an important one, especially here where there is community strife and power is solely in the hands of one side. In the name of security the British government has committed the blunders of internment, the torture and brutality of Holywood and Girdwood, the SAS, the Diplock courts, the Castlereagh beatings. This cruel will has spilled into prison affairs – condemnation of the innocent, excessive sentences, massive punishments during the prison protests, the debacle of letting the hunger strikers die. Now the young prisoners enter prison in the atmosphere of blackmail, informing, the corruption of legal procedures. The young in the Catholic community say all this is hypocrisy – how can you punish people for crimes and charge offenders if there is no change in society? They can only see a picture of punishment for punishment sake and short cuts through the law!

The young political prisoners today in the north of Ireland are from the ghetto. Their fathers and grandfathers had no loyalty to the 'Protestant government for a Protestant people'. Since 1969 the young people have even less loyalty to government. The physical conditions in which they live are deplorable. There is no employment. Joy riders and petty thieves, the product of their environment, are shot dead. What is the spill-over of this they see in the prisons? – long sentences, less bail (sometimes not even for pregnant women), excessive claustrophobic confinement.

The political failures have ensured the prison failures. The great symbol of all this at the present moment, the contempt of government for the human person, is the stripping naked of the girl prisoners.

The stripping naked of the women prisoners

Cruel, inhuman or degrading treatment is prohibited by the Universal Declaration of Human Rights. Stripping women naked has not only terrible physical effects but has terrible psychological effects. It crushes self-respect. It is counter-productive in every way. Normal people would not swagger about smiling and happy about such degradation. As a priest, I consider it to be contrary to the sixth and ninth commandments, a serious invasion of a woman's privacy and treating of the person as an object. It is shameful and cruel for the victim and the beholder to uncover a woman's private parts, to expose her genitals and anus to others, and a most dreadful thing to remove her sanitary towel. Remember the outcry at the degrading search of the Pakistani lady at Heathrow airport?

Past experience shows that cruel policies lay the foundations of further troubles. It is another failure, like the torture, like the SAS killings, like the plastic bullet maimings and killings, like the Shoot-to-Kill policy. It is terrible cruelty and what will the response to sound advice be? More punishment.

A positive policy

The May committee of 1979 had something positive to say. What it preaches, toning down the security mania, should be practised:–

> The purpose of detention of convicted prisoners shall be to keep them in custody which is both secure and yet pos-

itive, and to that end the behaviour of all the responsible authorities and staff towards them shall be such as to:

    (a) create an environment which can assist them to respond and contribute to society as positively as possible;

    (b) preserve and promote their self-respect;

    (c) minimise, to the degree of security necessary in each particular case, the harmful effects of their removal from normal life;

    (d) prepare them for and assist them on discharge *(par. 4.26)*.

In other words, the prisoner should be allowed to lead as normal a life as possible behind bars. The positive policy is there – why not work towards it? Attitude is important. The wise humane attitude allows, inevitably, warm social attitudes to develop. Fear has to be overcome, the fear in the name of security, of seeing people with some spirit, some happiness, some enjoyment, some normality. Loss of liberty is a great suffering in itself – every day a year – for prisoners, for families and local communities who often too hold the key to justice and peace. Now that prison uniform has been done away with, wasn't it stupid? Normality behind bars, as far as possible. There was a pervading truth behind the comedy series *Porridge*.

Normality in work and education too. Why not? Can the psychological barrier of the sewing of bags and uniforms, the mop, and the laundry (where would British prisons be without it?) not be overcome? Armagh Prison is a tiny little institution in our parish compared to our huge schools and the fact that each priest in the parish has the care of more than six hundred families. The physical organisation of decent work and education of such a small group could hardly tax the capability of the most average of persons. The girls are particularly expert at knitting, sewing, and crocheting. These are feminine things. It goes without saying that they could do more cooking.

Normality also means good physical conditions. The physical condition of Armagh Prison has always been poor but at least the prisoners used to have a fairly decent run about indoors. The present physical aspects of confined units seem fire hazardous and bad for the eyesight (the girls in A1 have no normal lighting). This confinement can be stultifying and boring and wastes human life. All prisoners should have open cells during the day. Long confinement in such cooped up conditions and even worse than that, extended cellular confinement, is cruel.

Attitude is important to embark on normalisation. What could happen in our social relationships? – Trust would break down if we regarded persons as objects, sneered at their anxieties and worries, caricatured them as 'hards' that must be broken, denied them any point of view, used our authority to mock, harass or persecute; communication would break down. If we take away a person's basic human rights, then how could we be surprised at just anger or non-communication? Prisoners too deserve normal human relationships. We should not fear the gospel message preached by Jesus concerning the degrading of the 'little ones'. Jesus broke the religious regulations of his day with such sermons. The authorities not only carpeted him for it. They crucified him.

Possibilities

The increase in parole is most welcome and especially the compassionate parole for long termers and those serving life. It has been of immense help to prisoners and their families. '24 hours' helps to assuage grief. (But imagine being stripped naked a few hours after burying your father?) Inter-jail visits – very good.

After 12 years of war and the prospect of another 12 to 20, it is clear that there must be a softening of heart all round to break the steady line of conflict. Forgiveness, love, kindness, must be shown by those with power. Not heaping up violence and guns. The trickle of releasing prisoners must start. The Republic of Ireland released 81 before Christmas. Did it even create notice or a stir? It would create a great stir of goodwill here. Sick prisoners, the young prisoners detained at the pleasure of the secretary of state who have already served long terms, women like Christine Smith, Etta Cowan, Pauline Derry and, of course, Christine Sheerin, who had received an atrocious long sentence and is in poor physical health and mental condition, the 'official' republicans in the compounds, all who have served long term terms (like Gusty Spence), should be released. As a beginning.

One would welcome dates of release for all prisoners. One welcomes the return to normalisation as regards the human, cultural and occupational interest of prisoners (Irish language, music, history, folklore).

Rights should replace the Victorian prison slang of 'privileges'. Never could I, of course, refer to prisoners by numbers. Or call them by the offensive term of RC, or worst of all 'inmates'. They are prisoners and they accept that reality.

There is an urgency about some things. It is more than shocking that there is still a protest going on in Armagh. Could an independent inquiry not find out why and sort it out within a few days?

On the horizon

What does one expect on the horizon? An independent element in the matter of complaints; unimpeded access to MPs; as much mail as one can afford; uncensored mail; the use of the telephone; the ending of the remand system except in the most serious of cases and the absolute avoidance of discussing the prisoner's charges which is his or her own affair while the case is pending; conjugal visits.

What above all would affect the Catholic community and the prison world to promote peace and justice? The restoration of full remission.

Oscar Wilde wrote in *The Ballad of Reading Gaol* (written while he was in prison):

This too I know – and wise it were
If each could know the same –

That every prison that men build
 Is built with bricks of shame,
And bound with bars lest Christ should see
 How men their brothers maim.

With bars they blur the gracious moon,
 And blind the goodly sun;
And they do well to hide their Hell,
 For in it things are done
That Son of God nor son of Man
 Ever should look upon!

May the Son of God visit us all with wisdom ...

Copy of letter of the Catholic priests of Armagh Parish to the
Governor of Armagh Prison, 30 October 1982

The Governor
Armagh Prison
Armagh

30 October 1982

Dear Governor,

Our primary responsibility above all others is to say Mass for
the prisoners in Armagh Prison.

Father Murray has been chaplain in Armagh prison for
the last 15 years. He must have complete control over the materials, vessels, vestments and books for all Masses celebrated
in the prison. It is his duty to see that the wine does not go
sour, which can happen quickly with an opened bottle that is
used once a week, and also to see that the breads do not go
stale. That is why we bring fresh breads and wine weekly to
the hospitals and prison where we celebrate Mass once a week.
The safest way of discharging this duty is to bring the mater-

ials in every week as has been done in Armagh Prison from time immemorial. It is our duty also to see that the bread and wine we use in Mass are procured from respectable suppliers who produce these items in accordance with the rigid strictures of the liturgy. This is best done if these materials are supplied through the parish who get them on a regular basis. Other arrangements (or failure to supply these items) are neither desirable nor helpful.

Regarding the sacred pyx – the pyx is a sacred vessel normally used to bring consecrated hosts to sick people. It is always treated with respect because the assumption is that it contains consecrated hosts or soon will. It is a vessel that the priest has responsibility for and it is inconceivable that a priest would use sacred vessels for an unlawful purpose. The priest also carries his oil-stocks for the anointing of the sick and we expect the same respect for this sacred vessel (one of our colleagues anointed a young man who had committed suicide in Long Kesh – he had his oil stocks with him when called in the emergency while he was in for Mass).

Unfortunately we are living in a sectarian state and the host itself and other sacred materials have been objects of mockery in public places. Catholic priests and people are particularly sensitive about the handling of sacred vessels and materials for Mass by non-Catholics.

We are also disturbed by the lack of freedom and spontaneity for the Catholic prisoners in regard to the sacrament of penance. Formerly the chapel was opened for confessions and those who wished to come exercised their freedom. There have been complaints from the girls that the restrictions that have crept in deter them from going to confessions.

Yours sincerely,

Fr Patrick McDonnell, Adm.
Fr Raymond Murray
Fr Patrick Campbell
Fr Patrick Finnegan
Fr Peter Kerr
Fr Richard Naughton

To: The Armagh Diocesan Senate of Priests

Armagh
14 December, 1982

Since 9 November 1982 a serious decline in standards of behaviour has taken place on the side of the authorities in the Northern Ireland Office prison affairs management. Girls entering or leaving the women's prison, Armagh, for whatever reason – admission to prison, going to and on return from remand court or for trial, visiting hospital, parole, inter-jail visits – have to undergo a completely naked visual examination of all parts of their body, front and back, while the prisoners stand totally naked before female prison warders. This type of inhuman degrading treatment has not been used during the fifteen years of my chaplaincy there nor in the seventeen years of my predecessor, Very Reverend James Clarke, PP. This new procedure has been a traumatic experience for young Catholic girls and older women, married and single, all of whom were reared and educated in Catholic houses and schools where the strictest standards of modesty were impressed upon them as a matter of conscience. This has now gone on for six weeks.

I give you an example: Geraldine Crawford, a young Catholic woman from the diocese of Down and Connor, was visually examined in this degrading way 13 times between the dates 20 and 30 November. The girls are made to turn around to be examined totally naked front and back.

I and my fellow priests consider this inhuman and degrading treatment contrary to Article 3 of the European Convention on Human Rights. As a priest I consider it to be contrary to the Sixth and Ninth Commandments, a serious invasion of a woman's privacy and treating of the person as an object.

No valid reason for this continuing disgraceful procedure has been brought forward by the secretary of state, Mr James

Prior, or the minister responsible for prisons in the north of Ireland, Lord Gowrie.

I want you to use your valuable influence to have this inhuman practice discontinued immediately.

Yours sincerely,

Raymond Murray

1983: THE REAL CONCRETE PERSON

Then Pilate's soldiers took Jesus into the governor's palace, and the whole company gathered round him. They stripped off his clothes and put a scarlet robe on him.

ST MATTHEW'S GOSPEL 27:27–28

Background to the political jails of Northern Ireland

Northern Ireland is a sectarian state; it will never work successfully; it will never have a permanent future. Sectarianism is so deeply ingrained into the mentality of those who administer its laws and systems that they cannot do so with fairness and equity. Some degree of fairness and justice can only be achieved by outside supervision, which, ironically, does come from the British in minuscule and irregular amounts. The first lesson and plea from the Catholic is that the British should do their duty and discharge their responsibilities to give equal rights to all as they have signally and deliberately failed to do since 1920, 1912, 1690 and 1608 in respect of the Catholic Irish.

One is sorry as a Christian to have to tell it as it is; it is a barbaric scene; but its roots go back to 1920, 1912, 1800 and 1690 – the great historical mistakes of the British in attempting to wipe off the map a people more ancient in history and in culture than themselves. The present day lesson for London and Dublin to learn is that the Catholics of Northern Ireland are a substantial people; in any new

Ireland they will demand power. The 'Troubles' are all about power.

One hears the comment often – 'There is no solution'. There are solutions and the first one is to be fair and decent and generous to the Catholic people. Everything has been tried – Special Powers acts, vicious discrimination in housing and jobs, internment many times, torture and cruel and inhuman treatment, Diplock courts, use of verbal statements and supergrasses, severe punishments in prisons, stripping prisoners naked, blackmail of young persons by 'security forces', semi-official assassinations and official 'Shoot-to-Kill' policies, stony-hearted and stony-faced government equally from the two parties in Britain. All this has not only failed but called forth ferocious and, may I say it, uncharacteristic violence in response.

Catholics in the north of Ireland would respond to kindness, generosity, forgiveness, considerate treatment. Why will the British government not use generosity and fair play to call forth an immediate response from the Catholics of the north?

The Protestant/unionist people know and the British government knows that any grant of justice, fair play, equality, to the fast growing Catholic population of the north will endanger the constitutional position, the border; and any kind of action, paramilitary, illegal governmental or oppressive governmental, is acceptable to repress the Catholics, and is tolerable and not to be condemned because it protects the Protestant monopoly of jobs in shipbuilding and aircraft building and heavy engineering, though these are subsidised by taxpayers' money, and the administration of 'Protestant' laws generally in favour of Protestants in cases of a political flavour. For example, in any case where the RUC or the British army or UDR are accused of killing persons with live or plastic bullets or treating persons in a brutal fashion in or out of custody (while on duty with official weapons), all these persons are acquitted if occasionally brought to trial. Prisoners, their families, the Catholic people, have to live with the proven fact that no member of the RUC or British army or UDR has served a sentence for killing or ill-treating persons, while on duty and using their official weapons, since 1969. This is what 'Protestant' law means in Northern Ireland – protect your security forces at all costs – they protect the border.

England has always used force to deal with the Irish. No attempt has been made to secure consent by generous treatment. It would not, of course, succeed in holding the border in the long run. But it would improve the situation quite dramatically. *Habeas Corpus* was suspended during the entire nineteenth century, except under Gladstone. And this pattern of repression has continued. Concessions will only be used when violence has ceased, the British say, instead of using concessions and fair play to bring violence to an end; no dialogue is pursued with the Catholic community – the British government and the Northern Ireland Office are as anxious to hold on to a 'Not an inch' policy as the DUP – so when people outside Sinn Féin want to open a dialogue on prison affairs and know that this would help to ease the general bad situation in the north, because of their experience with the relatives of prisoners, this gesture is scorned, every suggestion thrown out and further grievances caused by the stripping naked of women prisoners for visual examination. No sympathy is shown for the plight of the underdog; there is no generosity shown in the release of hundreds of young prisoners put in by questionable legal means; sentences are too long.

What is the time scale of violence now in 1984, and what does the present situation mean for the Catholic searching for an alternative and finding none that improves the situation? By religion the Catholic is committed above all to the sacredness of human life. The Catholic leader is committed to preventing young Catholics being involved in organisations which use murder and destruction to further their political aims. He is equally committed to preventing any person from being murdered, driven from home and business, harassed and held at checkpoints by the 'Date of Birth syndrome', arrested under false excuse, ill-treated illegally by agents of the law, falsely tried and thrown into prison for long periods on remand or in custody, beaten in prison or subjected to tyrannical severe punishments, long solitary periods, distinctions between prisoners based not on rights but on enticements and allurements; in short from being terrorised by illegal and several illegal groups alike. What alternative can he present to the people – especially to the poor Catholic ghetto people, if the British administration refuses to make any concessions, to release women prisoners like Bernadette Boyle who seems to be on the way to contracting anorexia nervosa (that would probably be the eighth victim of the psychological disease in recent years), Pauline Derry, the only remaining Special Category prisoner, Dolores O'Neill (who seems to have deteriorated very badly in health in the past two years) and Anne Bateson, who got ridiculous long sentences, Lorraine Halpenny who is withdrawn; to stop stripping women prisoners naked even when they are pregnant or having their periods; to release sick prisoners and those youngsters detained at the secretary of state's pleasure, prisoners falsely imprisoned by illegal methods, prisoners who have completely turned against violence as a means of political change.

Unless there is a change in British policy, unless they stop viewing the Catholic population through unionist eyes and balking at the Irish language, Irish music and literature, Irish nationalist ideas, Irish history, Catholic ethos be it moral theology, dogma, doctrines, ethics, homiletics; unless they stop viewing the Catholic population through unionist eyes which see the Catholics collectively guilty of every IRA/INLA atrocity; unless the British treat the Catholics in the north of Ireland with fairness and decency and forgiveness and restitution, the most average historian can only say that we must resign ourselves to unending and worsening violence. The young unemployed masses have no hope. They are excluded from political influence and power; the job discrimination is getting worse; legal oppression and illegal oppression is heavier; members of security forces are on charges of murder and people have the impression that little in that line has been uncovered; prisoners have brothers and relatives dead and in jail; they see the British government arm one side of the community and turn their forces completely into 'Protestant forces for a Protestant people'; they see the Orange marches and crowds enjoy the full support of British law bent to accommodate them; they see children killed by plastic bullets on the nationalist side. What can the Catholic Church offer them when there is no outlet for nationalist politicians and the SDLP are deliberately destroyed by Mr Prior by refusing to give them a share of power in the Assembly – the watershed that will lead to the final demise of the democratic SDLP in the local elections of 1985 – what physical force movement could ever have given democracy a greater blow than that?

More and more the Catholic community in the north of Ireland feels it is on its own. Alienation is growing very fast. There is no hope for dialogue. Partition east and west of the Bann is growing into a reality.

The Supergrass System

This is now affecting many prisoners. It is a perversion of justice and destructive of law. It removes the law as a protective shield for citizens. The community regards it as a climax to grievances of forced confessions, illegal procedures of interrogation, imprisonment without trial, verbal statements accepted. This use of supergrasses, placing grave fault on the judges, leads the nationalist community to cry, 'The courts are corrupt'. To interfere with the law is to sow grievances and suffering for many years to come. Women have been affected by it. They feel the law no longer protects them.

A false illusion is created that this is going to be a factor in ending violence. 'Short term gains are long term losses'. Advice on this matter will fall on deaf ears as with everything else. A sense of outrage and despair at the lack of fair play will prevail.

Stripping the women prisoners naked

The visual examination of the private parts of girl prisoners began on 9 November 1982, eased somewhat during 1983 due to the outrage felt by the Catholic Church in the north. But, as with everything else objected to from the Catholic Church in the north, the practice has continued. The minimum that Mr Prior has promised to the questions of Mr Kevin McNamara in the House of Commons is that the practice will be kept under review. No doubt the Catholic Church at home and abroad in the missions, the local bishops, and the Vatican will continue to be informed of this by the Help the Prisoners Organisation who regard it as inhuman, immoral, indecent, degrading, unchristian. Already it has been said that the British government, found guilty of cruel, inhuman and degrading treatment of Irish

Catholic prisoners by the European Court of Human Rights, has been using precisely that kind of treatment against women in Armagh Gaol by stripping them naked repeatedly without any meaningful cause and this happens even when women are pregnant or having their periods.

One calls to mind words in the Address of Pope Paul VI to the Diplomatic Corps 14 January 1978:

> From the cradle to the grave every human being, even the weakest and most under-privileged, deprived or left aside, possesses an element of nobility which is in the image of God and resemblance to him. And Jesus taught his disciples that his own Person is represented, particularly clearly, in the person of these poor people and these little ones.

Similarly Pope John Paul II in his encyclical, *Redemptor Hominis*, spoke how Christ united himself with each person:

> We are not dealing with the 'abstract' man but with 'each' man, for each one is included in the mystery of the redemption and with each one Christ has united himself for ever through this mystery. Every man comes into the world through being conceived in his mother's womb and being born of his mother, and precisely on account of the mystery of the redemption is entrusted to the solicitude of the Church. Her solicitude is about the whole man and is focused on him in an altogether special manner. The object of her care is man in his unique unrepeatable human reality, which keeps intact the image and likeness of God himself. The council points out this very fact when, speaking of that likeness, it recalls that 'man is the only creature on earth that God willed for itself'. Man as 'willed' by God, as 'chosen' by him from eternity and called, destined for grace and glory – this is 'each' man,

'the most concrete' man, 'the most real'; this is man in all the fullness of the mystery in which he has become a sharer in Jesus Christ, the mystery in which each one of the four thousand million human beings living on our planet has become a sharer from the moment he is conceived beneath the heart of his mother.

The whole import of the teaching of Christ is that he is mysteriously reflected in every human being. That is why he said, 'I was a stranger but you would not welcome me in your homes, naked but you would not clothe me: I was sick and in prison but you would not take care of me'.

Positive Points

One welcomes the extension of the home leave parole. Sometimes the first experience causes a psychological shock to the prisoner and it is difficult to face a return. But a second time round seems to work out much better.

One welcomes also the release of Etta Cowan and Christine Smith and one hopes that it heralds a similar policy towards prisoners like Bernadette Boyle, Lorraine Halpenny, Pauline Derry, Anne Bateson and Dolores O'Neill.

The restoration of lost remission during the protest is essential.

I would like to thank the Legion of Mary, the Society of Saint Vincent de Paul and the nuns of the convent, Armagh, for assistance during the year.

I pray that all priests entering Armagh Prison will always be free to preach the Gospel of Jesus Christ.

1984: A Voice in the Wilderness

In a context of alienation: 'Out! Out! Out!'
Prime Minister Margaret Thatcher to the Irish.[9]

PRIME MINISTER MARGARET THATCHER HAS declared to the Irish people north and south that there is no place for them in power sharing government in the six counties. Already Irish nationalists in the north are moving towards a *de facto* canton autonomy. They hesitated when Jim Prior, after 15 years of strife, refused to give them constitutional power sharing in his Assembly. But Prime Minister Thatcher's exclusion order, speedily backed by secretary of state Douglas Hurd, has left them in no doubt that there is no future for them in Northern Ireland politics. A distasteful scenario is now set, which means that as the Catholic nationalist 'canton' grows apart, it will seek natural power structures to accommodate reality, its own police and militia to balance the UDR and RUC in the British Protestant 'canton'. Romantic 'United Irish' nationalists for generations thought it might have been otherwise, but they have fast disappeared and the interests of the Orange and Masonic orders, which make up the official unionist party, anti-Catholic in nature, and the Paisley vote, which would never allow power-sharing, are now accepted. Catholics are out and they want to stay out. Mrs Thatcher's OUT OUT OUT and Mr Hurd's endorsement are accepted.

Mrs Thatcher's exclusion order is the logical political statement of the policy pursued by succeeding secretaries of state in Northern Ireland (Whitelaw excluded) and the Northern Ireland Office. They forced Irish Catholics in the six counties to become strangers in the state and outsiders in their own country. Over 15 years the prisons have been filled with political prisoners; there was the pogrom of 1969; internment 1971–75; torture and inhuman and degrading treatment of Catholics by the British army and RUC 1971–79 which filled domestic and international reports; illegal punishments and beatings of prisoners during the 'Blanket' protest; the needless deaths of the hunger strikers (which haunt us still like the *Belgrano* victims); the plastic bullet and 'Shoot-to-Kill' murders; now the newspapers carry the stories of statements concocted by RUC men in authority in murder cases involving the RUC; the comments of Judges McDermott and Gibson; the anti-Catholic behaviour of the UDR; the flagrant abuses of the PTA now undergoing an international scrutiny; the ugly cultural ignorance which would destroy Eamhain Macha. Mrs Thatcher's OUT OUT OUT sums it all up. It is accepted. Reality accepts *de facto* partition on the general line of the east and west of the Bann slogan. Another generation will have the job of working out the *de jure* logical consequences, the sins of the present hopeless British politicians.

Stripping naked the women in Armagh jail
The stripping naked of the women in Armagh, now the

main plank of Mr Nicholas Scott's prison policy, was introduced on 9 November 1982, shortly after a delegation from the 'Help the Prisoners' organisation, which included Cardinal Tomás Ó Fiaich, met Lord Gowrie and some civil servants. The delegation pointed out how a restoration of lost remission, releases of young prisoners sentenced at the secretary of state's pleasure, those who had completed long sentences, sick prisoners, special consideration for women, improvements on legal proceedings, education and meaningful work in prison, Irish magazines and journals, ending of degrading searching, would create a climate of peace. The answer was the stripping of women in Armagh Jail and two years of intense agony and strife, tension and alienation, such as the prison never before experienced. The stripping naked and visual examination of the women's anus and genitals is rejected on moral and security grounds. The mental suffering of the women, most of them Catholic and Irish, fits into the 'alienation context'. The policy pursued by the 'Help the Prisoners' organisation, namely the release of prisoners as a road to peace in Northern Ireland, we know, has been rejected and spurned. The hard men of the Northern Ireland Office have won their day. From a local point of view, I suppose one could say, it was symbolised in the refusal to release Pauline Derry before Christmas, a matter of a few days, after an 18 year sentence (on the grounds that an accelerated release would mean invoking the Prerogative of Mercy ... and Mercy is a bad word!!).

Release of prisoners rejected by Northern Ireland Office

Fr Denis Faul and I have, since October 1982, privately and publicly spread a philosophy that prisoners were a key to peace, knowing the pre-1969 prison situation, the releases of prisoners after the 1956 IRA campaign, but above all based on the knowledge of the Irish Catholic nationalist community. Our advice should have been accepted as a help to secretaries of state and ministers, and above all the personnel of the NIO who have no notion of the feelings, culture, history or thinking of Catholics. It would have meant a good substantial start: with the release of SOSPs, prisoners who had served 8–12 years; long term prisoners like Mairéad Farrell, Anne Bateson, Dolores O'Neill, Jeanette Griffith, Marian Clegg, Lorraine Halpenny, Eileen Morgan, etc; without any risk to the community (restoration of lost remission would send it on its way). The answer after two years is a vague rumbling that sometime somewhere in the distance something ... Is there a vested interest here – that the unionist community, RUC/UDR/Prison Services do not want violence to cease? Armagh Prison has more staff and outlay for less than 30 prisoners than St Catherine's College, Armagh, with a thousand high-spirited teenagers! The response had to be substantial and immediate to make an impact. We now join the SDLP in our community as voices crying in the desert.

The corruption of the courts

Catherine Moore was lately released after two and a half

years on remand. She was tried in a supergrass court. Supergrass courts are another form of internment. What would Britain do without imprisonment without justice? The courts were not only reduced to mockery by paid perjurers, but now we are faced with RUC men who have been told by superintendents to issue false statements ... and this is for the court where an oath is taken ... and by people in charge of the law. What a blow to the sense of British justice and the nonsense of the law as majestic and apart!

2,000 Catholics were interned in the period 1971–75. It continued in 1976–79 only the pattern was changed: the Castlereagh Interrogation Centre interned hundreds more through ill-treatment and forced confessions. Blackmail, threats, 'supergrasses' are the new conveyor belts.

A new spirit of fair play

One must congratulate the present authorities in Armagh Prison for the present good atmosphere and sense of fair play. Since October 1984 this spirit has prevailed among prison officers, prisoners and officials. There is no laxity on security but there is fair play, common sense and a human face. Long may it continue. The good or bad spirit in any community or institution is always breathed into it by those in charge. It is the spirit that counts.

The ending of stripping the women naked would remove the serious blight.

It should also be a much easier thing to provide more uplifting work for talented prisoners. The education schemes are a great advance. But could not more varied handwork be provided for the less academic?

The threat of instability

Looking back over 17 years of annual reports, without being too self-congratulatory, I am amazed at how prophetic they were. Their only usefulness, however, will be to serve as historical documents of the times.

It would be mad to think that their point of view might be considered, never mind acted on.

The spreading instability still and will threaten us. Power is at the root of all reconciliation; justice and power-sharing, not dominance. Enlightened politics are absent. The 'Out! Out! Out!' of Mrs Thatcher and Mr Hurd has guaranteed instability. The prisons will remain political. There is no hope.

1985: End of an Era

THE NORTHERN SIX COUNTIES WHICH make up Northern Ireland have in the past year moved towards *de facto* joint sovereignty, Britain and Ireland, with the Anglo-Irish accord. The substantial nationalist people, making up 40% of the adult population and 50% of the young people, have now a body to which they can refer their grievances. The political eruption of the past 15 years brought on by discrimination in housing, jobs, votes, civil and human rights, may now be alleviated. The FEA reports on Shorts, Mackies, the civil service and the building societies still indicate that a lot has to be done before discrimination ends; add the Sirocco works and the shipyard to that and one can understand why such matters occupy the papers in Northern Ireland. There will not be peace until there is social justice. The revolution of 1969 has left us with other problems that must be tackled. Whatever the evolutionary solution to Northern Ireland, these short term problems cause a lot of grievance. They ought to be remedied immediately. Security, the courts and the prisons are in this context.

Security

Part of the solution of the security problem will be a second police force to represent the nationalist community or canton. It is more and more evident as time goes on. There are many police forces in Britain and the forces here could be modelled on them. Opposition to this will wane as it is recognised that there are *de facto* two peoples with traditions that must be respected. The UDR, of course, will be phased out.

The Courts

The judges failed to protect the people from internment, imprisonment without trial. Over 2,000 Catholics were imprisoned from 1971 to 1975 for periods of one, two, three years, while the courts stood silent or supported this illegal oppression. Only two judges spoke up on specific cases of torture of detainees. The findings of the European Commission for Human Rights, the European Court of Human Rights and Amnesty International are an indictment of the judges in Northern Ireland.

The judges did not learn their lesson. They were silent on the torture and brutality that went on in Castlereagh Interrogation Centre from 1975–79. They convicted many persons solely on the basis of forced statements. Again Amnesty International and the Bennett Report of 1979 are an indictment of the lack of justice.

The judges of Northern Ireland went even so far as to accept verbal statements in court. The 'supergrass' development came after the Bennett Report. Obviously there was a policy that certain nationalists must be imprisoned. This was easy while imprisonment without trial existed and later with the Castleragh brutality. After the Bennett Report the number of blackmail cases from Castlereagh Interrogat-

113

ion Centre increased dramatically. This led into the 'supergrass' scenario. Now, unfortunately, the courts in Northern Ireland are held in disdain by the populace. This 'supergrass' system, far from fitting into the law's role of protecting the citizen's right to liberty and life, is a perversion of justice and destructive of law. It resembles internment where persons were put into prison on the suspicion, prejudice or dislike of state agents and officials. People are now sent to prison on the uncorroborated evidence of persons of dubious character who may have committed serious crimes or may have committed perjury. The judges are gravely at fault in accepting such 'supergrass' evidence. How can one judge deal with involved cases of many people charged on many counts – churchmen, statesmen, lawyers are now asking – are they even listening to the evidence? 'Supergrasses' are a source of pity – they are held incommunicado by the RUC from friends and relatives. They can be carefully rehearsed for many months. They are specially confined in prison. They and their afflicted and suffering families must be helped with compassion. 'Supergrasses' are victims of a situation created by the tyranny of the state. The result of the 'supergrass' system, aimed at the nationalist community (it falls down in the loyalist cases) is that the term 'law and order' is a mockery in Northern Ireland. The law crawls in humble submission before crown, privilege and money. The 'supergrass' system must be ended immediately, otherwise it is clear to the public that there are no rights, no justice, no fair play in Northern Ireland.

The judges must be increased in number, half drawn from the nationalist community and half from the British community. Three judges in the present Diplock system are a necessity. The public expects judges to do their duty, not to be a source of ridicule and contempt in the community, not to be seen as political hacks without honour.

Prisons

A remarkable feature of the past five years is the steady decline in the number of prisoners in all the prisons. This is in complete contrast to the policy worked out by the Northern Ireland Office. Maghaberry has lain waste and vacant for years. It had been thought that the state needed more and more prisons. The opposite is the case. They can close some of them. Armagh Prison is a good example of that. There are only 20 political prisoners left and this with the floating population of the few ordinary prisoners is a very small prison population indeed. And yet a huge institution with governors, ranks, offices, trades is maintained in a ratio of eight to one, staff to prisoners. At a time when there is so much talk of 'cuts' in expenditure, this surely must be a major scandal – 'money for the boys and girls?' Six more political prisoners will get out in 1986. The prison will soon return to the pre-1969 period when only a few women prisoners were in prison. Only by spreading prisoners over all wings and floors is a semblance made of an excuse for such huge staff. What justifies round the clock staffing for one floor of a wing with one or no prisoner?

For four years the 'Help the Prisoners' committee urged the steady release of prisoners as a move towards peace in the community. It wasn't taken up. Like Rhodesia and South Africa the urge to generosity and to a softer line that would encourage peace was not accepted. The restoration of full lost remission after the hunger strike is an example of lost opportunity. People were arbitrarily divided into 'conforming' and 'hard-line' prisoners. Nobody benefited. The only example of mercy was when the secretary of state, Douglas Hurd, stepped over the civil servants to release a few prisoners. He left and the policy was not pursued. It has taken four years of public pressure to make the Northern Ireland Office give dates to some of those sentenced at the secretary of state's pleasure – some have been in jail for 13 years (two such from my parish). Can there be hope of a more liberal policy, or are releases connected with 'holding hostages' or maintaining 'material' for prison industry?

Stripping Irish Catholic women naked
Since the Ballykelly 'Hooded Men', prisoners are not forced to wear masks. The white noise and amphetamine drugs have disappeared. Prisoners are no longer submitted to flogging – the first piece of legislation passed by the Belfast government was known as the Flogging Act – prisoners were tied to a triangle and flogged in Crumlin Road Jail (*cf. Facts and Figures of the Belfast Pogrom 1920–22* by G. B. Kenna). We can put the beatings, forced baths and forced

haircuts of Long Kesh behind us. The crank and the tread wheel go back to Victorian times, thank God. But surely the stripping naked and visual examination of the private parts of the Irish Catholic girls housed in Armagh Prison is a severe blow to any contemporary penal reformers? These girls will go down in history as victims. When everything else is forgotten about Lord Gowrie and Nicholas Scott this degradation will be linked with their names, for not having the courage to over-rule the civil servant or civil servants who insist on it.

Another distressing factor in Armagh Prison is long-term confinement for one offence. All loss of association for more than a week should go before a visiting board well-staffed by independent people.

Stripping girls naked, long 'lock-ups' belong to a penal system that does not go beyond the custodial and punitive mentality.

Conclusion

This is probably my last report. The lack of numbers hardly justifies Armagh as a prison institution. Since 1984 the atmosphere viz-a-viz staff and prisoners has improved due to a more understanding direction. This is to be welcomed. In the wider context it is up to the politicians to move towards partnership and equal power sharing. It would be a bleak future if this tiny piece of land was to be convulsed by another volcano of suffering.

The lesson is clear. Generosity and compassion always pay off! Is there a possibility?

EPILOGUE

WHEN THE WOMEN WERE REMOVED to Maghaberry Prison in the vicinity of the Maze in March 1986 the authorities continued the same policy as in Armagh, a concerted campaign to integrate all types of prisoners and to assert tight control over the political prisoners especially. The new women's prison was relatively small compared to Armagh Prison and was built beside a large prison for men where a similar policy of integration was being pursued, although in the case of the men there was a choice to go to Maghaberry or stay in the Maze (Long Kesh). Segregation and oppressive control led to antagonism between officers and prisoners. An easing of tension only occurred when in 1988 there was a governor who could wisely give and take and was prepared to listen to the prisoners. Then there was some improvement.

In the new prison the non-conforming politicals were broken up into small groups and spread over several wings, six in B One, five in B Two, four remands in D One and two in D Two. Other prisoners were in A One and A Two. Such a division hindered healthy human relationships. The prisoners needed more stimulation in company where association was larger and more free. There was severe restriction on movement. Once prisoners left the cells and the bathroom area and entered the association and kitchen area they were cut off by a grill and could not re-enter. Similarly for outside recreation in the yard, the choice lay between being locked in the cell or staying outside whatever the weather. Prisoners only assembled together at Mass.

Strip searching as in Armagh continued and brought suffering to the prisoners and their families. On 2 March 1992 a horrific incident occurred when, against their will, twenty-two women were stripped naked in their cells in a major search of the prison. The women had been informed that a search of the prison was to take place and that they would not be unlocked. Later they were informed that each would be subjected to a strip search. They were threatened with loss of remission and solitary confinement if they did not comply with the order. The stripping took place over ten hours. Male officers dressed in riot gear with batons and shields stood by while up to eight female officers entered each cell. The prisoners were seized and dragged to the floor; their faces were pushed tightly into the ground so that they could not see and their mouths were covered to stifle their screams. They were then stripped naked. Until 2 March a routine search involved a thorough 'rub-down' of a fully clothed prisoner. Resistance led to forced stripping by officers. The prisoners argued that to allow this new form of stripping them naked in their cells would start a precedent. This stripping raid, the ensuing punishments and legal consultations of the aggrieved women poisoned relations between guards and prisoners.

From 1986 to 1997 the women prisoners in Maghaberry

carried on an intense campaign to chip away at injustices. They opposed the limited number allowed to associate, the doubling of searches going on visits, the tiny cramped visiting space, the long walk of visitors from the car to the prison, strip searching, the general meagre programme of education and other facilities offered to them in comparison to the ample opportunities offered to men in the neighbouring prison who, in the interest of an integrated regime, were being wooed by more acceptable conditions. There seemed to be an attitude that like provision for the small number of women did not warrant the expense. Although met from an uncaring attitude on the part of the Northern Ireland Office, who did not want to discuss the problems with the prisoners, and the stubborn attitude of some of the prison authorities, the women gradually brought results by their constant insistence on rights and their legal action on the grounds of sex discrimination. The legal action was settled out of court. Education facilities were improved, association wings enlarged and there is less strip searching. They raised the serious questions of parole, the status of temporarily transferred prisoners from England, and conjugal visits. They still campaign to have certain conditions on a par with the men in Maghaberry, especially lock-up which has been abolished for all prisoners in Long Kesh and for the men prisoners in Lagan House, Maghaberry. They still call for equal provision with men prisoners for education, access to telephones, a proper surfaced exercise yard, and gym equipment. Another discrimination case is beginning.

The document of the Second Vatican Council entitled *The Church in the Modern World* states, 'It is up to public and private organisations to be at the service of the dignity and destiny of humankind; let them spare no effort to banish every vestige of social and political activity and to safeguard basic human rights under every political system'. Monsignor Denis Faul and I once wrote:

> Whatever makes a human being more a human being helps that person achieve a greater degree of unity with the Creator through Christ, God made man – this is the true and essential meaning of the Incarnation which shapes and dominates the lives of the ministers of Christ. This is true humanism. In the life of the prison chaplain this spirit of Christian humanism takes on a particular sharpness because it may bring the priest into direct critical confrontation with the agents of the state. The chaplain may find persons entrusted to his charge who are being made lesser people by such a system in prison so that their personality and health, physical and mental, are being destroyed by shapeless and ugly clothes, by mindless discipline, by meaningless work, by prolonged detention and overlong imprisonment. The essential spark of hope, the human initiative, the development of responsibility and maturity may be deliberately inhibited. If a system does this it is an immoral system – it makes a human being less a human being; it destroys God-given qualities; the chaplain will have to fight against it, work against it with the weapons of the spirit. He may be sacked for opposing the state as Father Gott was in England.[10] He may have to stand up against ecclesiastical superiors. But he will have the satisfaction of avoiding the dreadful sight, common in the twentieth century, of the representative of Christ's Church washing his hands along with the representative of Caesar while one of these 'little ones'

121

who are Christ goes to be crucified by neglect or malice or an inhuman application of Victorian standards.

NOTES

1   The women painted political and religious themes on white handkerchiefs with felt pens as souvenirs for friends.

2   Prisoners who alleged assault. Previously, on 3 May 1972, John Hume had been given permission to visit John Carlin in Long Kesh along with a doctor. A further assault on Cyril Canning in Long Kesh on 18 December 1972 in Compound 6 is described in Faul, Murray, *Whitelaw's Tribunals* (1973).

3   Timothy Davey, a 14 year-old English boy was sentenced to six years and three months and fined over £4,000 on a drugs charge in Turkey in February 1972. His case merited an editorial in *The Times* on 1 March 1972.

4   Patrick Crawford, an internee, was found hanged in a compound in Long Kesh prison camp on 3 June 1973; it appears that he took his own life. On 26 December 1973, George Hyde, 19 years of age, was found dead from injuries in a loyalist compound at Long Kesh; other prisoners in the compound were transferred to Crumlin Road Prison, Belfast, pending an inquiry; no one was charged with his murder.

5   Dolours and Marion Price, with eight others, were charged on 12 March 1973 with conspiring to cause explosions in London on 8 March 1973. They were jailed for life and went on hunger strike at the end of November 1973 for transfer to prison in Northern Ireland. The were artificially forcibly fed from 3 December 1973 to 18 May 1974. Hugh Feeney and Gerard Kelly, imprisoned with them, also went on hunger strike. On 8 June 1974 all four ended their hunger strike after 206 days. On 13 December 1974 the sisters were transferred from Brixton Prison to Durham. On 18 March 1975 it was announced that they had been transferred to Armagh Prison.

6   The republican internees set fire to long Kesh Prison Camp on the evening of 15 October 1974. An account of the fire is given in Faul, Murray, *The Flames of Long Kesh* (1974).

7   Special tribunals were set up in Long Kesh to enquire into cases of those detained (interned). See Faul, Murray *Whitelaw's Tribunals* (1974).

8 NIACRO – Northern Ireland Association for the Care and Resettlement of Offenders.

9 After a two-day Anglo-Irish summit at Chequers, the Prime Minister, Mrs Margaret Thatcher, on 19 November 1984 rejected the three options advanced by the New Ireland Forum: a unitary state, a federal state, a federal Ireland and joint authority. It became known as the 'Out! Out! Out!' speech.

10 Fr Gott had protested against the cruelty of controlled units in English prisons. He was forced to leave the prison service in England. For Control Units see *Whose discretion? Fairness and flexibility in the penal ststem*, The Howard League for Penal Reform, 1974/1975, pp. 5–6; Martin Wright, *Making Good: Prisons, Punishment and Beyond* (Burnett Books, 1982), pp. 57–8; Mick Ryan, *The Politics of Penal Reform* (Longman, London and New York, 1983), pp. 48–9; Mike Maguire, Jon Vagg, Rod Morgan, eds *Accountability and prisons: Opening up a closed world* (Tavistock Publications, London and New York, 1985); 'Williams *v* Home Office (No. 2)' in *All England Law Reports*, 1981, pp. 1211–1248.

THE SAS IN IRELAND

RAYMOND MURRAY

The SAS in Ireland traces the history of the British Army Special Air Services Regiment, the SAS, in Ireland over the past twenty years. It details their activities – intelligence gathering and surveillance, their links with British Intelligence, notably MI5 and MI6, their connection with sectarian murders and many other deaths.

Fr Raymond Murray is a respected commentator on events in the north of Ireland. In this book he analyses in detail the activities of the SAS and plain clothes soldiers in the Six Counties. His research leads him to the conclusion that in many instances the SAS engaged in a careful and organised shoot-to-kill policy.

No Faith in the System
A Search for Justice

Sr Sarah Clarke

Paddy Hill of the Birmingham Six described Sister Sarah Clarke as *the Joan of Arc of prisoners*. This book tells her story from her childhood through the period she spent as a teacher of art in the Bower convent in Athlone and finally to her work with prisoners in British jails. Over a period of twenty-five years, Sister Sarah relentlessly pursued the cause of justice on behalf of Irish people arrested under the Prevention of Terrorism Act. In 1976 she gave up her teaching job to do full-time pastoral work with prisoners and their families. Among the thousands of prisoners with whom she worked were the Birmingham Six, the Guildford Four and the Maguire Seven. Her campaigning work frequently resulted in clashes with the Home Office and she was eventually barred from visiting prisoners but continued her work outside the prisons with wives and children of the prisoners.

This book is a testimony to the determination and courage of a woman who for many years was at odds with both the Church and State because of her perception of the appalling failings of the British criminal justice system.

Democracy Denied

Desmond Wilson

The name of Des Wilson has always meant two things: integrity and controversy. The diocesan priest whose mission to Ballymurphy, one of West Belfast's poorest ghettos, caused him to try an alternative theology and reject the irrelevant instructions of his bishops, has now turned an informed eye upon the 'Northern situation'.

The author's challenging, anti-establishment analysis of the history of the six counties in the past hundred years demands a close reading and evaluation at the highest level. He argues that all British governments have deliberately manipulated both Protestants and Catholics for their own economic purposes and that the Dublin government and the Church have co-operated in the matter. This contention, argued with compelling logic, cries out for a rebuttal.

In this essential commentary the more complicated issues of Irish politics, including the undiminished support for the IRA and the question of decommissioning, are examined from a fresh point of view.